Obeyed

A 33-Day Devotional to Reclaim Peace, Stop Striving, and Walk in Divine Alignment

Prisca Noronha

NORONHA PUBLISHING

Published by Noronha Publishing

ISBN: 978-93-5717-515-9 (eBook)

ISBN: 978-93-5759-379-3 (Paperback)

ISBN: 978-93-5768-896-3 (Hardcover)

Disclaimer: This book is intended for educational, inspirational, spiritual encouragement and informational purposes only. It does not replace professional, legal, medical, psychological or mental health advice. Readers should consult a qualified health care professional where appropriate. The author and publisher disclaim any liability arising from the use of this book.

First Edition: 2026

Published in India.

For My Parents,

Who taught me that life may wobble, but God's promises stand steadfast. Thank you for steering me to trust, obey, and embrace His perfect timing.

CONTENTS

The Case for Obedience

We live in a world that teaches people how to pursue outcomes, but rarely how to align their hearts. Many voices promise success through formulas, manifestation techniques, or mindset hacks. They teach people to chase results, control outcomes, and speak things into existence.

Yet few ask the deeper question: ***"Who am I becoming while I pursue what I want?"***

Obedience may not be a popular word in a culture that celebrates self-direction. Yet throughout Scripture, surrender to God's voice is where clarity, growth, and transformation begin.

This book is for anyone caught between striving and surrender, ambition and alignment, faith and control, as it does not promise shortcuts to blessings. It offers a pathway to alignment.

It is for the person who:

- ✓ Experiences a deep spiritual longing yet feels weary of the hype.
- ✓ Wants direction more than quick results.
- ✓ Desires a life shaped by God, not goals.
- ✓ Is learning to trust timing instead of forcing outcomes.

Every day calls you to simple, real-life surrender. This builds character, calms emotions, and strengthens faith.

Because a life aligned with God is not built in dramatic moments — it is built through daily choices.

This is not about attracting what you want. It is about becoming who God is forming you to be.

Introduction

Remember a time when life felt full of possibility—when the future seemed open and hopeful. It was a childhood dream. The joy of getting what you wanted. Learning to ride a bike, winning a race, or feeling proud as you enter a new stage of life. In those moments, you didn't just feel happy—you felt settled as if you stood precisely where you were meant to be.

Somewhere along the way, that clarity began to fade. Dreams took longer to reach. Opportunities stalled. You put in hard work, made careful plans, and prayed with deep sincerity. Still, the results didn't always match your effort. Frustration often crept in quietly, appearing as confusion, fatigue, or a subtle unease. You might sense you did your best, but the path ahead still felt unclear.

Over time, we tighten our grip by planning more, pushing harder, and trying to control timing. Yet effort without alignment leads to exhaustion. It is possible to be busy and still be off-course.

What we often lose is not possibility, but direction. And direction cannot be forced—it must be followed. The weight of striving is real, but it is not permanent. Alignment restores what pressure cannot.

There were seasons in my life when I chose to be quiet before God, even though I didn't have the right questions to ask Him, and my own answers weren't working. Some prayers felt like they hit the ceiling and came back unanswered. Nothing dramatic happened. No sudden voice. No instant clarity. But over time, a pattern emerged.

The right seasons often followed small acts of surrender. These were times when doors opened, and everything fell into place. Not perfect alignment—just honest steps taken when I sensed God's direction.

That realisation was uncomfortable. I saw that I was faithful in belief, but selective in response. I followed instructions when they felt reasonable or convenient. But when trust required waiting, humility, or unseen service, I hesitated. Sometimes, I delayed acting. Other times, I tried to force outcomes. Even though force moved the situation, there was never peace.

We don't refuse God outright—we negotiate. We follow the parts that suit us and quietly label the rest as "discernment" or "waiting." But delayed surrender is still disobedience. Isaiah 1:19 states it plainly:

"If you are willing and obedient, you shall eat the good of the land."

This verse wasn't new to me. I read it as a child. But as life grew complex and responsibilities increased, its meaning matured. To a child, obedience may sound like compliance. To an adult, it becomes a strategy for living.

Willingness and obedience are not separate—they work together. Alignment is not about intense effort; it is about consistent response. Once I understood this, obedience stopped feeling like a rule and became a way of life.

A leader builds discipline, and an athlete shows commitment. Similarly, surrender shapes daily choices. The question slowly shifts from: "What do I feel like doing?" to "What is aligned?" And when that shift occurs, decisions become simpler.

Direction clarifies. Peace grows steadier.

How Obedience Unlocks Your Life

Obedience goes beyond simply following rules — it is the posture that unlocks your deepest desires. It aligns your actions with God's timing and purpose. When you choose to surrender in small, unseen ways, you prepare for results that hard work alone cannot achieve.

Think of it like planting seeds in the right soil. Growth cannot be forced. You water, tend, and wait, trusting the process that governs the harvest. Your desires — success, peace, love, clarity — begin to grow when your choices stay aligned with the right path.

Obedience does not restrict you; it refines you. Alignment eases tension and helps you receive what you long for — not by forcing outcomes, but by finding calm in God's timing.

Alignment is learned, practised, processed, and lived out.

How This Guide Works

This book is designed to move obedience from intention to instinct. In the days ahead, you won't just learn principles — you'll practice them daily. Each entry combines reflection, real-life examples, and intentional actions. Step by step, a rhythm forms that reshapes how you respond, decide, and move forward.

This journey has a clear, intentional rhythm, and the path unfolds in 6 themes:

Part I — Awakening to Obedience
Part II — Surrender & Realignment
Part III — Practising Obedience Daily
Part IV — Deep Inner Alignment
Part V — Stewardship, Impact & Multiplication
Part VI — Beyond the Journey

Your 33-day journey with a roadmap:

16 Days of Focused Topics
1 Day to Pause and Reflect
16 Days of Focused Topics

Like building blocks, small acts of surrender compound over time. By the end of this book, obedience won't just feel like a duty — it will become a natural way of making choices.

How to Use This Book Daily for Maximum Impact

To experience the full fruit of obedience, engage with this journey intentionally. This is not meant to be rushed — it is a daily practice that shapes you over time.

- ***Set aside quiet time:*** Spend 10–15 minutes each morning without distractions. Reflect on what you've read and complete the daily steps. Consistency matters more than duration.
- ***Engage with the story:*** Place yourself in the shoes of the biblical figure mentioned and ask honestly, "Would I respond the same way?"
- ***Answer honestly:*** Use a dedicated journal for the reflection questions. Writing often reveals what silent reflection alone can miss.
- ***Act on what you learn:*** Complete the daily steps. Action turns insight into lived alignment. Even a small step, repeated, builds momentum.
- ***Build the rhythm:*** Each day connects to the previous one. Review your notes to see how tiny acts of surrender influence your choices.

Before you begin Day 1, make a simple decision: show up honestly each day, even when progress feels quiet. This journey requires participation.

Obedience grows through practice, not pressure.
Alignment deepens through rhythm, not rush.

PART I — AWAKENING TO OBEDIENCE

Day 1 - What Obedience Truly Is

Obedience is the spiritual "manual override" for a life that feels stuck. We wait for confidence before taking a step, but momentum rarely comes from feelings—it comes from movement. Taking the first step without a full map doesn't erase uncertainty, but it does silence paralysis.

Just like a GPS, obedience gives directions one turn at a time. If you miss a turn, it recalibrates. But it cannot guide someone who never leaves the parking lot. In the same way, God's guidance unfolds as you move.

This shows up in our everyday life:

- You sense a nudge to reach out to someone, but you wait until you feel "ready."
- You pray for clarity, but ignore the last instruction you already received.
- You ask for direction, but postpone the step right in front of you.

Sometimes you are not waiting on God—God is waiting on your first step. This tension between movement and clarity is not new.

Throughout Scripture, God often invited people to move before they fully understood, and Abraham's story reminds us of this. Born in Ur of the Chaldeans, he lived in a culture shaped by idolatry until God called him to leave everything familiar behind.

When Abraham was 75 years of age, God commanded him:

"Go from your country, your people and your father's household to the land I will show you." — Genesis 12:1

Without hesitation, Abraham stepped out to a destination unknown, trusting the voice of God over the details.

At this time, Sarah, his wife, was barren, but God promised them descendants as numerous as the stars.

"The Lord appeared to Abram and said, 'To your offspring I will give this land.' So, he built an altar there to the Lord, who had appeared to him." — Genesis 12:7

Decades passed before the promise was fulfilled. At 90 years of age, Sarah gave birth to a son and called him Isaac as instructed.

Later, Abraham's obedience was tested again when God asked him to sacrifice Isaac. He prepared to obey, but God intervened and provided a ram instead.

Imagine the weight of such obedience: leaving behind the comfort of family traditions, familiar streets, the security of a known future, waiting decades for a child or being asked to surrender that which we love the most. From a human perspective, it appeared reckless. Yet, from the perspective of faith, it was alignment.

Abraham trusted the voice of God above all other details, from the destination to the outcome. He obeyed before clarity arrived, and that obedience became the seed of a lasting legacy.

As part of God's covenant, they were renamed. Abram became Abraham ("father of many nations"), and Sarai became Sarah ("princess"), signifying their new identity in God's plan. Their obedience shaped not only their lives but the destiny of nations.

Here are a few ways to listen and follow God:

- ***Pause to Listen:*** Create intentional silence in your day. Even five minutes of stillness can open space for God's whisper.
- ***Notice the Nudge:*** Pay attention to small impressions, gentle convictions, or repeated thoughts that align with Scripture.
- ***Test with Truth:*** Compare what you sense with God's Word. Obedience is never outside His character or commands.
- ***Take the First Step:*** Act on what you've heard, even if it feels small or incomplete. Movement breaks paralysis.
- ***Release Control:*** Let go of the demand for a full map. Trust that clarity will unfold as you walk.

- ***Recalibrate Quickly:*** If you miss a step, don't spiral into guilt. Like a GPS, God redirects. Return to obedience without delay.
- ***Celebrate Momentum:*** Notice how obedience brings peace, clarity, or unexpected provision. Gratitude reinforces trust.

The Cost:

1. Letting go of your demand to know everything in advance.
2. Releasing the comfort of control.
3. Acting before you feel fully ready.

The Value:

1. Clarity that unfolds step by step.
2. Momentum that replaces stagnation.
3. A direction you could never design on your own.

Reflection:

1. Where in your life are you waiting for a complete map before you are willing to move?
2. What fear, comfort, or desire for control might be influencing your delay?
3. What is one small step you sense God may already be inviting you to take?

Today's Step:

1. Identify one nudge or instruction you have been delaying because you do not have all the answers.
2. Take that one step today—send the message, make the call, or begin the task.

3. Do it intentionally, and notice whether your internal fog begins to lift.

Guidance meets you on the road of obedience, not in the parking lot of hesitation.

Day 2 - Expressing Your True Intentions

Vague desires often lead to vague direction. You cannot align your life with a target you refuse to define. Honesty is the first rule of obedience because God meets us in truth, not performance. Be honest about what you want. This brings clarity to your prayers and purpose to your actions.

We desire "God's will," but secretly hope it aligns with our comfort. Others ask for change while protecting the habits that keep them the same. Clarity begins when you stop giving spiritual answers and start giving honest ones.

Imagine an archer, standing on a vast, open field with a bow in hand and a quiver full of arrows. They have the strength to draw the string and the skill to release, but there is no target in sight.

If they fire now, the arrow is not flying with purpose—it is simply wandering. It might land in the grass or strike a stone, but it can never be called accurate because there was no intended mark.

We live our spiritual lives this way: we have the energy and the desire for change, but we refuse to name exactly what we want. We pray for "blessing" or "guidance" in generalities, effectively shooting arrows into an empty sky.

Honesty is the act of stepping up to the line and firmly planting a target in the ground. When you name your true intention—whether it is a specific healing, a career shift, or a broken relationship—you give your obedience a place to land.

An archer who refuses to name the target isn't being "flexible"; they are being aimless. Alignment begins the moment you stop firing at the wind and start aiming at the truth.

This often shows up in everyday moments. You say you want growth, but avoid the conversations that stretch you. You pray for opportunity but hesitate when responsibility comes. You ask for direction but keep your real desires hidden, even from yourself.

Scripture shows that clarity often comes before transformation. Blind Bartimaeus demonstrated this when he encountered Jesus on the roadside near Jericho. Though surrounded by a crowd and urged to be quiet, he kept calling out for mercy.

When Jesus called him, Bartimaeus tossed aside his cloak, jumped up, and went to Him. Then Jesus asked him a direct question:

"'What do you want me to do for you?' The blind man said, 'Rabbi, I want to see.'" — Mark 10:51

Jesus already knew he was blind, yet He still asked. Clarity matters. Bartimaeus did not hide behind vague words. He named his desire plainly. His answer revealed faith, focus, and readiness. He was not only hoping for change, but he was also prepared to receive it.

Bartimaeus regained his sight and then chose to follow Jesus along the road. His clarity did not end with a miracle; it continued into obedience. He teaches us that clarity is both the doorway to breakthrough and the foundation for discipleship.

Here are a few ways to express your true intentions:

- ***Pray with honesty:*** Begin with an open heart before God, speaking truthfully about your feelings and needs.
- ***Be transparent:*** Lay bare your intentions, bringing even hidden parts of your heart into His light.
- ***Revelation of motive:*** Invite God to uncover the deeper reasons behind your desires and reshape them to reflect His will.
- ***Exposure:*** Present your inner drivers (motivations, impulses, or hidden intentions) honestly, welcoming His guidance to redirect them toward what is good.
- ***Surrender your intentions:*** Hand over both pure and imperfect intentions to God in faith, allowing Him to transform them for His purposes.
- ***Daily Realignment:*** Refocus your mind on God throughout the day whenever distractions arise.

- ***Persistence:*** Continue in prayer faithfully, like Bartimaeus, even when discouraged or delayed.

The Cost:

1. Admitting what you truly want.
2. Letting go of safe, noncommittal answers.
3. Risking vulnerability by being specific.

The Value:

1. Focused direction instead of scattered effort.
2. Prayers that reflect your real heart.
3. Alignment between desire and obedience.

Reflection:

1. What do your daily choices reveal you truly want, beyond what you say?
2. Where might you be giving safe answers instead of honest ones?
3. What desire have you been hesitant to name before God?

Today's Step:

1. Write down your number one desire for this journey. Be honest, not spiritual-sounding.
2. Name what you truly hope will change, grow, or become clear.
3. Then ask yourself: "Am I willing to obey the steps that may be required to reach this?"

What you name with honesty, you can pursue with purpose.

Day 3 - Clearing the Noise

Noise is one of the greatest disruptors of alignment. This does not only mean sound, but includes constant input, endless opinions, internal worries, digital distractions, and mental chatter that fills every quiet space.

Noise is anything that distracts you and makes it hard to notice God's guidance.

The challenge with obedience is not rebellion—it's distraction. God's guidance is often gentle, and a busy mind can easily miss it. When your inner world is crowded, even a clear direction can feel far away.

Imagine standing in a famous museum gallery, positioned directly in front of a timeless masterpiece. You have come to study the details, the brushstrokes, and the light. But the room is crowded. Tourists are shouting, cameras are flashing, and the floor is vibrating with the heavy footsteps of people rushing toward the next exhibit.

In this environment, you don't need the museum to turn on more lights to see the art; you need the noise of the crowd to fade. You need the room to go silent so your focus can sharpen.

Guidance from God works similarly. It isn't that His voice is missing; it's that the room of your life is too loud. Digital pings, endless opinions, and the internal chatter of worry act like a noisy crowd pushing past you.

Clearing the noise isn't about finding new information; it's about curating your environment. To see the art of God's direction, you must intentionally step back from the crowd. Stillness is the gallery wall that protects the masterpiece of His voice from the world's chaos. You cannot hear the whisper of the Spirit if you are shouting back at the noise of the day.

Have you ever tried to pray only to find your mind drifting to your to-do list? Or listened to someone speak while mentally forming your reply?

We fill our moments with constant sound or activity to keep us occupied. And so, we may hear God's words but miss the meaning unless we listen intentionally.

Scripture shows that learning to listen is part of learning to obey. Samuel was the miracle child of Hannah, born after years of her prayers and tears.

In gratitude, she dedicated him to the Lord's service, and from a young age, he lived in the temple under the care of the prophet Eli.

Though still a boy, Samuel's life was already marked by devotion and service to God.

When God first called Samuel, he didn't recognise God's voice. He assumed Eli was calling him and ran to him several times. Finally, Eli understood what was happening and told Samuel how to respond. When the Lord called again, Samuel answered:

"The Lord came and stood there, calling as at the other times, "Samuel! Samuel!" Then Samuel said, "Speak, for your servant is listening." — 1 Samuel 3:10

When Samuel finally listened, God revealed a sobering word: judgment was coming upon Eli's household. Eli's sons had dishonoured God, and Eli had failed to restrain them. The Lord declared that their guilt would never be atoned for by sacrifice or offering.

Samuel was afraid to share this message, but Eli urged him not to hide anything. With trembling honesty, Samuel told him everything. Eli received it humbly, saying, *"He is the Lord; let Him do what is good in His eyes."*

Samuel's turning point wasn't that God spoke louder—it was that Samuel became quieter. He shifted from running in confusion to standing in attentiveness. His posture of listening opened the door for God to entrust him with the truth that would shape a nation.

This moment marked the beginning of Samuel's prophetic ministry. From then on, the Lord was with him, and none of his words fell to the ground. All Israel recognised Samuel as a prophet of the Lord.

Samuel's story is our mirror. We often miss God's voice not because He isn't speaking, but because our lives are too loud. The noise of constant input, notifications, opinions, and worries drowns out His whisper.

Here are a few ways to clear the noise:

- ***Create Space for Silence:*** Pause today and whisper, *"Speak, Lord, your servant is listening".*
- ***Shift Posture, Not Volume:*** God doesn't shout; He waits for your attention. Listening is about focus, not noise.
- ***Limit Competing Voices:*** Silence notifications, step away from constant commentary, and let Scripture be the loudest voice.
- ***Practise Stillness Daily:*** Build small rhythms of quiet into your routine, even five minutes at a time.
- ***Let Obedience Grow from Listening:*** When His voice is clear, your words and actions carry weight.
- ***Recalibrate Quickly:*** If you drift back into noise, return without guilt. Like Samuel, simply say again: *"Speak, Lord."*

The clarity you long for isn't found in louder answers; it is found in quieter living. Samuel's destiny began when he silenced the noise and listened. You can too.

The Cost:

1. Letting go of constant input.
2. Choosing quiet when noise feels normal.
3. Making space when busyness feels easier.

The Value:

1. A heart that recognises God's prompting.
2. Clarity that comes from stillness.
3. Direction that is received, not forced.

Reflection:

1. What most often distracts you during quiet moments?
2. When does your mind feel most crowded or rushed?
3. Where could you create a small space for stillness this week?

Today's Step:

1. Set a timer for ten minutes today. Sit without your phone, music, or tasks. Let your thoughts settle without chasing them.
2. Say this simple prayer: "Speak, Lord, your servant is listening."
3. Notice what surfaces when the noise fades. Write down any thought that brings clarity or conviction.

Clarity grows where noise fades.

Day 4 - Stop Forcing Outcomes

Striving and alignment move in opposite directions. When you push for outcomes before their time, you can harm the very thing you are hoping for. Obedience is not passive; it is faithful co-operation with God's timing.

Peace begins to grow when you focus on doing what is right and release the results. When you loosen your grip on outcomes, you create space for God to work.

Imagine a master potter sitting before a rapidly spinning wheel with a lump of raw, unformed clay. A novice might try to force the clay into shape, using jerky movements and aggressive strength. But the harder they push, the more the clay resists, eventually wobbling off-centre until it collapses into a shapeless mess. The novice ends up with wet hands and an empty wheel.

The master potter works differently. They don't fight the spinning wheel; they partner with its momentum. They apply a steady, patient pressure that is almost invisible to the eye. The clay doesn't feel forced; it feels guided. It rises into a beautiful vessel not because of the potter's force, but because of the potter's alignment. Peace is the steady hand on the wheel of God's timing.

When you try to force an outcome, rush a decision, manipulate a person, or chase a result, you become the novice jerking the clay. You end up with a mess and an empty heart. But when you stop forcing and start aligning, you discover an unforced power. You realise that the spinning wheel of your life is not there to destroy you, but to help you rise. Your role is not to power the wheel, but to stay steady in the Hands that do.

We notice this tension in our day-to-day activities. We rush decisions, chase quick answers, or try to secure results too soon. We replay situations in our minds, trying to solve what has not yet unfolded. Striving rarely brings clarity; it usually brings pressure.

The Bible gives a tender picture of this in Hannah's story. She longed deeply for a child and carried that ache for years. Her sorrow was visible and heavy. Yet, instead of closing her heart, Hannah brought her pain honestly before the Lord.

She prayed quietly and with great intensity. The priest Eli saw her and thought she was drunk. Hannah told the priest she wasn't drunk but very troubled and was pouring out her soul in prayer.

Her words came from anguish, not performance. Hannah was not trying to force an answer; she was releasing her burden. Her prayer was not polished; it was real. She named her grief and placed it before God.

Eli understood her pain and spoke peace into her life, as he hoped her request would be granted.

After that moment, something shifted in Hannah; her face was no longer downcast. Even though her circumstances had not changed instantly, her heart had. Peace arrived before the answer did.

"In the course of time, Hannah became pregnant and gave birth to a son. She named him Samuel." — 1 Samuel 1:20

Hannah recognised Samuel as an answer to prayer. But she didn't cling to him in fear or try to control what came next. Instead, she honoured her vow and dedicated him back to the Lord. What she received as a gift, she returned in trust.

That act is powerful: she didn't just celebrate the outcome, she surrendered it. Hannah shows us that true peace doesn't come from holding tightly to what we've been given, but from releasing it into God's hands.

Hannah's posture is a model for us. We often try to grip outcomes tightly—relationships, careers, finances, even spiritual growth—thinking that control will secure them. But forcing outcomes usually creates anxiety, not peace. Hannah teaches us another way.

Here are a few ways to stop forcing outcomes:

- ***Shift from Grasping to Giving:*** What you receive as a gift, return in trust.
- ***Find Peace Before the Answer:*** Release your burden honestly, and let peace arrive before circumstances change.

- ***Practice Surrender Daily:*** Surrender isn't weakness; it's choosing to trust God with what you cannot control.
- ***Celebrate Obedience, Not Results:*** Joy grows when you focus on faithfulness rather than outcomes.
- ***Release Pressure:*** Striving rarely brings clarity; it usually brings anxiety. Let God's timing shape what is beautiful.

The clarity here is simple but life-changing: peace grows when striving slows. Hannah's story shows us that surrender is not weakness—it is strength. She stopped forcing outcomes by releasing her deepest desire into God's faithful hands. And in doing so, she discovered peace before the answer and joy after it.

What you receive as a gift, return in trust. Stop forcing outcomes, and let God's timing shape something beautiful in your life.

The Cost:

1. Letting go of the need to control timing.
2. Releasing the belief that pressure creates results.
3. Trusting when pushing feels easier.

The Value:

1. Peace that is not tied to outcomes.
2. Choices shaped by trust instead of fear.
3. Results that unfold at the right time.

Reflection:

1. Where do you feel pressure to make something happen right now?
2. What are you trying to control that is beyond your responsibility?
3. What might change if you focused on obedience instead of results?

Today's Step:

1. Choose one situation you have been worrying about or trying to control.
2. For the next hour, whenever it comes to mind, pray: "I will be faithful in my part and trust God with the outcome."
3. Notice how your thoughts shift when control loosens.

Peace grows where striving slows.

PART II — SURRENDER & REALIGNMENT

Day 5 - Trusting Timing You Don't Control

We often measure the success of our lives by the speed of our progress. When a door remains closed, or a prayer goes unanswered for years, our natural inclination is to label it a failure or a "wall."

We treat time as an enemy to be conquered rather than a tool used by God. To understand obedience in a season of waiting, we must first accept that our vantage point is naturally restricted. We are viewing the "how" and the "when" of our lives through a very narrow lens.

Imagine standing behind a massive, towering loom where a Master Weaver is at work. From your perspective, the back of the tapestry is a chaotic tangle of loose ends, frayed knots, and dark, overlapping threads. It looks like a mess of wasted time and poorly chosen colours. If you were in charge, you would likely cut those threads or force them into a different order.

But the Master Weaver is not looking at the back. He is seated on the other side, focused on the front. What you call a tangled knot, the Weaver calls a secure anchor. What you see as a dark, ugly thread, the Weaver sees as the necessary shadow that gives the golden highlights their brilliance.

Trusting timing is the humility to admit that you are standing on the wrong side of the loom. You are judging the unfinished back of the work while God is crafting the masterpiece on the front. Delay is not the Weaver being slow; it is the Weaver carefully pulling a specific golden thread through the dark places. You do not need to see the whole pattern to stay aligned—you only need to trust that the Weaver has not dropped a single stitch.

The hardest part is not the waiting, but the silence. We often confuse God's silence with His absence, or His stillness with His indifference. However, in the economy of Heaven, silence is not a void; it is a profound form of communication.

When God is silent, He is often working on the crux of your soul—your motives, your endurance, and your hidden pride. He is quiet not because He has left the room, but because He is completing a work so deep that noise would only be a distraction.

The Master Weaver is most quiet during the most critical part of the pattern, and God's silence is often the sign of His closest proximity.

Joseph's life shows what it looks like to live on the "backside of the tapestry" for years. As a teenager, he received dreams pointing to leadership and influence—he saw the "front side" of the design early. Yet those promises were followed by betrayal, slavery, and prison.

For thirteen years, he lived in places where he had no control over timing, outcome, or even his own voice.

From a prison cell, his life looked like a mess of frayed knots.

However, the "back side" of the tapestry tells a different story of proximity:

"The Lord was with Joseph so that he prospered, and he lived in the house of his Egyptian master." — Genesis 39:2

Even in slavery and later in prison, the text repeats: "The Lord was with him." Joseph could not hear a "voice" telling him when he would be free, but he could sense the divine "presence" that kept him faithful.

He exercised his obedience by trusting God's timing when he couldn't control the calendar.

"But while Joseph was there in the prison, the Lord was with him; he showed him kindness and granted him favour." — Genesis 39:20–21

Scripture tells us Joseph was thirty years old when he finally entered Pharaoh's service. Those thirteen years of "dark threads" were not wasted; they were the very threads that built the wisdom, resilience, and discernment required to save nations. Each hidden season trained him for the visible one.

When the time came, the Master Weaver revealed the front of the tapestry: Joseph wasn't just a survivor; he was a leader prepared to sustain a world through famine. And so, not only was he ready to rise—but to lead well.

We often measure progress by speed and visible results, assuming delay means failure. But Joseph's years in slavery and prison remind us that waiting seasons are not wasted seasons. What looked like knots and shadows on the backside of the tapestry were, in fact, the very threads God was weaving to prepare him for leadership.

Here are a few ways to trust God's timing:

- ***Release Control:*** Acknowledge that the calendar and outcomes are not in your hands, but in God's.
- ***Shift Perspective:*** Remember you are viewing the "backside of the tapestry," while God sees the masterpiece from the front.
- ***Embrace Silence:*** Accept that God's silence is not absence but deep work within your soul.
- ***Anchor in Presence:*** Like Joseph, trust that "the Lord is with you" even in hidden seasons.
- ***Reframe Delay:*** See waiting not as wasted time but as preparation for future responsibility.
- ***Cultivate Patience:*** Allow endurance to grow, knowing speed can spoil what God is forming.
- ***Trust the Weaver:*** Rest in the assurance that not a single thread of your life is misplaced in His design.

The Cost:

1. Releasing your personal timeline and the demand for a "status update."

2. Letting go of the need for quick proof of progress.
3. Accepting that God's silence is a sign of His work, not His departure.

The Value:

1. Deep roots that can sustain the weight of future influence.
2. A character that is "concert-ready" for high responsibility.
3. The peace of knowing the Weaver is at the controls.

Reflection:

1. Where are you currently judging the "back side" of the tapestry instead of trusting the Weaver?
2. How would your anxiety shift if you viewed God's silence as His "surgical focus" on your heart?
3. What might this season be forming in you that speed would have spoiled?

Today's Step:

1. Identify one area where you've been "shouting" at God for an answer. Choose to be silent with Him for ten minutes.
2. Do not ask for a map; acknowledge the Weaver.
3. Write down three things this 'season of wait' has taught you that you could not have learned in a season of speed.

What feels like a delay is often divine protection in disguise.

Day 6 - The Internal Cost of Obedience

Obedience isn't free; it often requires a down payment of pride, comfort, or the need for approval. These costs feel personal because they strike at our need for security. Yet, what feels like loss is actually growth in disguise. Obedience reshapes the heart long before it changes the circumstances.

Growth is rarely cosy. Imagine a child wearing their favourite coat. It is familiar, warm, and has fit them perfectly for years. But as the child grows, the coat that once provided security begins to feel like a cage. The sleeves are too short, the shoulders are tight, and the buttons strain against the slightest movement.

The coat hasn't changed, but the child has. To remain in the old coat is to choose restriction over reach, a choice that ultimately stunts us. Surrender is the act of leaving the "safe" behind to make room for something stronger.

When God calls you to a new level of alignment, your old habits, old friendships, and old ways of "forcing" outcomes start to feel tight. They pinch your spirit. This discomfort isn't a sign that you are failing; it is the evidence that you are expanding.

The "Internal Cost" is the willingness to take off the old coat—even if you loved it—to make room for the new identity God is draping over your shoulders. You cannot experience the freedom of a new season if you are still trying to breathe in the fabric of the old one. Growth requires the courage to be uncomfortable for a season so you can be aligned for a lifetime.

We may spot this as an inner push to be honest, to set boundaries, or to make a tough choice. But we hesitate, as we fear judgment and how others perceive us. That very pressure point often reveals where growth is needed.

Esther's life is a masterclass in this internal cost. She didn't ask for power; she was placed in a palace by circumstances beyond her control, finding comfort and security in her royal status. Then came the crisis. A royal decree threatened the Jewish people with destruction.

Esther's cousin, Mordecai, urged her to intervene. But the cost was high: approaching the king without an invitation meant a potential death sentence. Even as Queen, Esther wasn't exempt from the law. Mordecai's challenge reframed her fear:

> *"And who knows but that you have come to your royal position for such a time as this?" — Esther 4:14*

Esther chose courage over comfort. After three days of fasting and prayer, she moved with wisdom rather than impulse. She didn't just rush in; she waited for the right moment to speak with humility. Her obedience may have cost her the safety of the palace walls, but it fulfilled her calling and rescued her people.

Here are a few ways to embrace the internal cost of obedience:

- ***Recognise the Pinch of Growth:*** Notice where old habits, comforts, or identities feel restrictive. Discomfort is often the sign of expansion.
- ***Release the Old Coat:*** Let go of familiar patterns that no longer fit. What once felt safe may now be limiting.
- ***Choose Courage Over Comfort:*** Like Esther, step into risk when obedience requires it. Fear of perception must not outweigh faithfulness.
- ***Practise Honest Surrender:*** Admit where you are tempted to cling to approval or security, and place those desires in God's hands.
- ***Align with God's Timing:*** Move with wisdom, not impulse. Obedience is steady cooperation with His plan, not forced outcomes.
- ***Celebrate Character, Not Ease:*** Value the growth of your heart over the comfort of your circumstances. Obedience reshapes you before it reshapes the situation.

The Cost:

1. Letting go of the familiar.
2. Releasing the "coat" of safety.
3. Choosing to be courageous over comfort.

The Value:

1. The freedom to move in a new season.
2. A life no longer constricted by old patterns.

3. A character that can carry royal responsibility.

Reflection:

1. What comfort or habit might you be outgrowing right now?
2. Where are you hesitating due to the fear of people's reactions?
3. What might courage look like in your current situation?

Today's Step:

1. Identify one specific area where you feel the "pinch" of spiritual growth.
2. Today, intentionally step out of that old comfort zone.
3. Whether it's making a difficult call or letting go of a defensive attitude, choose the discomfort of expansion over the safety of the cage.

Growth often begins where comfort ends.

Day 7 - Continuing When Nothing Changes

The most perilous stage of any spiritual journey isn't the beginning, where excitement carries you, or the end, where the finish line is in sight. It is the middle—the vast, quiet stretch where your effort is high but the evidence is zero.

We are a culture of "updates" and "notifications"; we expect a ping of progress for every ounce of input. When a door remains shut despite your faithfulness, discouragement doesn't usually arrive with a bang; it takes root in the silence.

You begin to wonder if your obedience is actually working, or if you've simply been spinning your wheels in a void. We often mistake a lack of visible movement for a lack of divine momentum.

In this digital age, we have forgotten how to labour without a "like" or a "share" from the world around us, leading us to believe that if no one is watching—not even God—then nothing is happening.

But in Part II of this journey, we must learn that the most critical growth happens underground before the first sprout ever breaks the surface. True alignment is forged in the seasons where you feel forgotten. Stopping now isn't just quitting; it's walking away from a harvest that has already been paid for by your persistence.

Imagine a concert violinist preparing for a world-class performance. For months, they sit in a room alone, repeating the same three-bar phrase hundreds of times.

To a casual observer, it looks redundant—even mind-numbing. There is no applause, no stage lights, and often the musicians themselves cannot hear a difference between the thousandth and the thousand-and-first repetition.

However, inside the musician's body, muscle memory is being perfected. Every "boring" repetition is building the neural pathways and internal tension required for the music to eventually flow without effort. If the musician stops because they feel bored, the concert will never happen.

The silence of the practice room is not a lack of progress; it is the precision of preparation. If you judge the skill by the performance alone, you miss the masterpiece being built in the mundane hours of practice.

Noah's life is the ultimate testament to the "muscle memory" of obedience. When God told Noah to build an ark for a coming flood, He wasn't giving him a construction project but a one-hundred-year endurance test.

For over a century, Noah's obedience had no environmental confirmation. There were no clouds, no rising tides, and no weather reports to validate his labour.

Every hammer blow echoed in a world that thought he was a fool.

Noah had to show up to the "practice room" every single day, building a solution for a problem that hadn't arrived yet.

"By faith Noah, when warned about things not yet seen, in holy fear built an ark to save his family. By his faith, he condemned the world and became heir of the righteousness that is in keeping with faith." — Hebrews 11:7

Noah didn't build the ark because the hands of the clock were moving; he built it because he was calibrated to a different frequency.

A hundred years passed with no visible change to the human eye, but behind the scenes, the gears were turning.

When the windows of heaven finally opened, Noah wasn't scrambling to get ready; he was already set in his posture. His long-term discipline in the drought is exactly what allowed him to survive the deluge.

His story proves that God doesn't wait for the storm to start the work; He uses the quiet of the drought to build the character that will weather the weight of the breakthrough.

Here are a few ways to continue when nothing changes:

- ***Redefine Progress:*** Notice where growth is happening within you, even if circumstances look unchanged. Write down one unseen way you've grown (patience, trust, consistency).
- ***Practise Relentless Obedience:*** Keep doing the daily act of faith you've been given, even when it feels repetitive. Choose one task today and complete it with care.
- ***Break Free from Validation:*** Stop checking for signs, applause, or updates. Instead, pray once today without looking for immediate confirmation, trusting God hears you.
- ***Build Unshakable Resilience:*** Repeat one spiritual discipline (prayer, Scripture reading, journaling) with focus, treating it as training that strengthens endurance.
- ***Anchor in God's Timing:*** When impatience rises, speak aloud: "God's silence is preparation, not absence." Use this truth to reset your perspective and steady your trust.
- ***Celebrate Hidden Strength*:** At the end of the day, reflect on one way waiting has made you stronger. For example, if you've grown calmer in stress or more consistent in prayer, thank God for that hidden victory before asking for visible change.

The Cost:

1. Releasing the dopamine hit of immediate "status updates" from God.
2. Continuing to "hammer" when the sky remains perfectly blue.
3. Accepting that boring consistency is often the highest form of worship.

The Value:

1. A heart that is "concert-ready" for high-pressure responsibility.
2. Integrity, which is formed when there is no audience to applaud your progress.
3. The ability to stand firm in a storm because you did the work in the sun.

Reflection:

1. Where in your life are you judging the "concert" because the music hasn't started yet?
2. What "muscle memory" (patience, grit, secret prayer) is God building in you through this repetition?
3. If you knew the "rain" was coming in ten years, would you be frustrated by today's silence, or would you use it to hammer more firmly?

Today's Step:

1. Identify one area where you are tempted to quit because it feels boring or redundant.
2. Today, perform that task with the meticulous care of a musician in a practice room. Don't look for the audience; focus on the precision of the stroke.

3. Write down one way your character has strengthened specifically because things haven't changed yet.

Don't quit in the silence—the hands move only when the gears are set.

Day 8 - Obedience of the Tongue: Aligning Your Words with Your Calling

Words are small, but they carry direction. Many lives are steered more by what is spoken than by what is planned. Obedience of the tongue means matching your words with your actions. It is possible to pray faithfully yet speak carelessly; to believe deeply yet talk negatively. The tongue often reveals what the heart is still learning.

Imagine a high-altitude reservoir sitting deep within a mountain range. It holds millions of gallons of water—potential energy that can power an entire city. This power is only useful because of the massive, silent dam that holds it back. If the gates are left wide open, the water rushes out in a frantic flood, wasting its energy in a single, destructive moment. The valley below is overwhelmed, and the reservoir is left empty.

However, when the gates are opened only by a master engineer's command, the water is released with precision. It is channelled through turbines to create constant, steady power. Stewardship is the wisdom to keep the gate closed when the urge to vent is at its highest.

Obedience of the tongue is the spiritual dam of your life. Every time you feel a nudge from God or have a new vision, it is like fresh water entering your reservoir. If you speak it too soon, you bleed out the "pressure" required to actually build it. When you vent in anger, you are simply "dumping" your potential energy into a conflict that has no future. Your words should be the turbines that power your purpose, not the leaks that drain your strength. Scripture is direct about the weight of our speech:

"The tongue has the power of life and death, and those who love it will eat its fruit." — Proverbs 18:21

Speech is never neutral; it shapes the atmosphere of your life. Jesus warned that the tongue is the primary indicator of your internal alignment:

"For the mouth speaks what the heart is full of." — Matthew 12:34

Many struggles begin with speech. Gossip weakens unity. Harsh words wound deeply. Speaking ill of parents or authority hardens the heart. Constant negative language trains the mind toward defeat. Even sharing your plans too early can drain focus and invite distraction.

Use this in your day-to-day activity:

- Instead of saying, "I always fail at this," start saying, "I am learning to do this better."
- Instead of announcing every project, work in silence until it has structure. Early exposure drains the pressure needed for progress.
- Instead of venting in anger, pause. Guard your "gates." A moment of silence preserves hours of peace.

- Instead of gossip, let silence do its work. If a word isn't true, necessary, and kind, keep the gate closed.

Here are a few ways to work on obedience of the tongue:

- **Choose Restraint Over Reaction —** When you feel pressure to vent, pause before speaking. Hold silence for a moment and let the urge pass before responding.
- **Speak The Truth Over Exaggeration —** Replace dramatic or negative statements with accurate, constructive words. For example, say "I am learning" instead of "I always fail."
- **Offer Encouragement Over Criticism —** Intentionally encourage someone who needs it, instead of pointing out flaws.
- **Guard Timing Over Impulse —** Keep new ideas, visions, or goals private until they are structured. Resist the urge to announce them prematurely.
- **Filter Words Through Purpose —** Before speaking, ask: "Is this true, necessary, and kind?" If not, keep the gate closed.
- **Align Speech with Faith —** Let your words reflect what you believe. Speak hope, not defeat; speak life, not despair.

The Cost:

1. Choosing the "pressure" of silence over the relief of venting.
2. Restraining the impulse to prove yourself or announce your "wins."

3. Managing your potential energy by guarding your private matters.

The Value:

1. A life powered by steady, focused conviction.
2. A reputation for wisdom and calculated strength.
3. Protection over your vision while it is building its vitals.

Reflection:

1. Are your current words "powering" your future or just "leaking" your energy?
2. Which situation lately made you want to "open the gates" of your tongue in anger or pride?
3. How would your influence change if people knew you only spoke when the "Master Engineer" gave the signal?

Today's Step:

1. Identify one area of your life where you feel "high pressure"—a new idea, a frustration, or a secret goal.
2. Commit to keeping the gate closed today. Do not speak of it. Let the pressure build into a focused plan.
3. Notice how much more energy you have for the task when you don't spend it on the talk.

A guarded tongue does not limit you—it protects your power.

Day 9 - Obedience as a Habit: Replacing Old Patterns with Aligned Ones

Habits shape direction more than intentions do. A single decision rarely defines a life, but repeated choices do. Alignment is strongest when it shifts from a strenuous act into a daily habit. This change replaces harmful cycles with aligned ones.

Imagine standing at the edge of a thick, overgrown jungle. To reach the other side for the first time, you must hack through vines and fight for every inch of progress. It is slow and exhausting. This is what obedience feels like on Day 1—it is a gruelling struggle against the overgrowth of your old nature.

However, if you walk that same path every day, the grass stays flat. If you lay stones down, the footing becomes sure. Eventually, once the path is paved, you no longer have to "think" about where to step; your feet move by instinct. A habit is simply a path you have travelled so many times that the resistance has been removed.

Destructive habits are like old, broken roads that lead to a dead end. They are easy to travel on because they are already paved, but they are taking you to the wrong destination. You don't have to fight for direction when you've already paved the way.

In today's world, destructive habits take many forms: constant scrolling to escape reality, harsh speech, drinking to numb stress, or sexual compromise to fill emotional gaps. Many of these begin as temporary relief but solidify into permanent routines.

Jesus illustrated this in the story of the Prodigal Son, who found himself on a broken road that ended in a pigpen. The turning point came when he recognised the pattern:

"When he came to his senses..." — Luke 15:17

His return home began with a decision to realign. Change starts the moment you name the old pattern and commit to the "machete work" of a new trail. Obedience interrupts the cycle.

Here are a few ways to overcome and replace unwanted habits:

- ***Start with Awareness:*** Name the habit or pattern that is misaligned. Write it down honestly; recognition is the doorway to change.
- ***Replace, Don't Just Remove:*** Choose a new aligned action to fill the gap. For example, replace scrolling with prayer, or harsh words with silence.
- ***Fill the Space with What Helps:*** Intentionally choose life-giving alternatives: prayer over panic, movement over stillness, conversation over isolation.
- ***Reduce Access to Triggers:*** Create distance from what feeds the old habit. Limit exposure, set boundaries, and steward your environment wisely.

- ***Build Small Daily Obedience:*** Commit to one repeated act of obedience each day. Lay a "stone" on your new path with every choice.
- ***Invite Accountability:*** Share your commitment with someone trustworthy. Let their support strengthen your resolve when old roads feel easier.
- ***Return Quickly When You Slip:*** Don't stay in the "pigpen." When you drift, realign immediately. Obedience is not perfection, but faster returning.

The Cost:

1. The exhausting "machete work" of hacking through the vines of an old identity
2. Releasing the "easy travel" of a broken road that leads to a dead end.
3. Trading the temporary relief of a routine for the long-term discipline of a realignment.

The Value:

1. A cleared trail where your "Yes" to God no longer feels like a struggle, but a natural flow.
2. A "paved" character that remains steady and durable even when life's weather turns harsh.
3. Reclaiming the mental energy once wasted on fighting old patterns, now used to power your purpose.

Reflection:

1. Which habit in your life are you still travelling on, simply because it is a path that's already paved, familiar, and feels "easy"?

2. What specific "overgrowth"—a habit, a thought pattern, or a digital distraction—needs to be hacked away today to clear your new path?
3. If you continue on your current most-travelled road for five more years, does it lead to the "Father's House" or back to the "Pigpen"?

Today's Step:

1. Identify one habit you want to replace, not just remove.
2. Choose one small obedient action you will repeat daily this week in its place.
3. Every time you perform that action, you lay a stone on your new road. Small daily obedience rebuilds what reckless patterns once broke.

A life aligned is not built in a day. It is paved one step at a time.

PART III — PRACTICING OBEDIENCE DAILY

Day 10 - Obedience Without Motivation

Feelings are fleeting, but obedience is a firm choice. If we only move when we feel inspired, our lives will be as unstable as our moods. Often, the strength we are waiting for doesn't show up until we take the first step. Faith-driven action doesn't rely on existing energy; it generates it.

Imagine an athlete committed to a rigorous training program. It's 5:00 AM on a cold, rainy Tuesday. The bed is warm, the room is dark, and every emotion is screaming to hit the snooze button. There is zero "motivation" to go outside and run through the mud.

The athlete doesn't go because they feel excited; they go because they made a commitment when they were dry and rested. The first few minutes are miserable—the air is biting, and the body feels heavy. But a mile into the run, something shifts. The blood starts to pump, the lungs open up, and the focus returns. The energy followed the action. Had they waited to "feel like it," they would still be in bed, losing ground.

Obedience is showing up to the field when the weather of your emotions is working against you.

This pattern of "action before feeling" is etched into the story of the Widow of Zarephath.

God instructed Elijah to go to Zarephath, where a widow would provide him food. When Elijah arrived, he asked the widow for water and bread. She explained that she had only a small amount of flour and oil left—just enough to prepare a final meal for herself and her son before they expected to die of hunger.

In that fragile moment, Elijah asked her to do the unthinkable:

"Don't be afraid. Go home and do as you have said. But first make a small loaf of bread for me from what you have and bring it to me, and then make something for yourself and your son. For this is what the Lord, the God of Israel, says: 'The jar of flour will not be used up and the jug of oil will not run dry until the day the Lord sends rain on the land.'"

This wasn't an inspiring request; it was a demand for total surrender during a crisis. Imagine being asked to give away your last meal or the last few pennies you have left during a time of need. For most, self-preservation would feel natural.

Yet despite her dire circumstances, the widow obeyed Elijah's instructions. And God miraculously sustained her household: the flour and oil never ran out, providing daily food for Elijah, the woman, and her family.

Notice that the miracle didn't start until her hands moved.

Here are a few ways to work on demotivation:

- ***Move Before You Feel Ready:*** Begin the task even when emotions resist. Set a timer for five minutes and start; energy often follows action.
- ***Choose Commitment Over Comfort:*** Act on the decision you made in clarity, not the mood you feel in the moment. Let your "Yes" guide you, not your feelings.
- ***Trust That Strength Will Arrive Mid-Step:*** Recall past times when energy returned once you began. Use that memory to fuel today's obedience.
- ***Silence the Survival Instinct:*** When obedience feels risky, remind yourself that God's instruction is safer than self-preservation. Speak His promise aloud.
- ***Anchor in Faith, Not Inspiration:*** Pray before acting, asking God to steady your will. Then move forward even if motivation hasn't appeared.
- ***Celebrate the Shift After Action:*** Reflect on how your mindset has changed since you started. Thank God for the strength that met you in motion.

The Cost:

1. Moving when you feel tired, uninspired, or emotionally "heavy.
2. Letting go of the demand to feel "ready" or "confident" before acting.
3. Choosing the instruction over your own survival instincts (Self-Preservation).

The Value:

1. A strength that only awakens once you are in motion.
2. Consistency shaped by faith, making you reliable even when your mood is not.
3. A life guided by a steady commitment rather than the rising and falling tides of emotion.

Reflection:

1. What specific responsibility are you currently "snoozing" because you are waiting for a feeling of inspiration that hasn't arrived?
2. Recall a time when you started a task you dreaded, only to find that your focus and energy returned halfway through. How can that memory fuel your "Yes" today?
3. If God asked you to give from your "last handful" today, would you wait to feel motivated, or would you move from trust?

Today's Step:

1. Choose one responsibility you have been postponing because you don't "feel" like doing it.
2. Set a timer for five minutes and just start. Do not pressure yourself to finish the whole thing; just get on the field.
3. Notice how your mindset shifts once the "blood starts pumping."

Obedience is a decision, not a mood.

Day 11 - Obedience Without an Audience

Obedience without an audience shifts the heart from seeking approval to seeking alignment. What is practised in private determines what can be sustained in public. Many people crave influence, but it is quiet faithfulness that builds the internal structure required to carry it.

Think of a bowl of dough that has just been kneaded with yeast. To the naked eye, the dough looks completely inactive. It is covered with a heavy cloth and placed in a quiet, dark corner of the kitchen. From the outside, for a long time, it appears entirely unchanged.

However, within that silence, a slow and powerful process is unfolding. The yeast is producing gas that stretches and strengthens the invisible gluten network from within, expanding its structure and preparing it to rise.

If the baker grows impatient and rushes the dough into the oven too soon, the bread will never reach its fullness; it will be dense, heavy, and underdeveloped.

Hidden time is not wasted time—it is the mandate for internal expansion. Your private integrity is the yeast of your character. It works in the quiet corners of your life so that you are structurally sound enough to handle the heat of your future.

Integrity is the secret rhythm of choosing what is right when the audience is zero.

- It is being honest when the books will never be audited.
- It is keeping a promise when no one is there to applaud.
- Forgiving when the other person doesn't even know they've been forgiven.

You cannot be trusted to stand in the spotlight until you have mastered the alignment of the shadows. Daniel's life reflects this kind of obedience.

Long before he was a high-ranking official, he had a private rhythm of prayer. It wasn't a performance; it was a lifeline.

When a decree was signed making prayer illegal, punishable by death in a lion's den, Daniel didn't change his behaviour to be dramatic. He simply continued the same quiet habit he had practised for years in his private room.

The officials were jealous of him and searched for a way to trap him. They realised the only way to accuse Daniel was through his devotion to God.

> *"He was faithful, and no corruption was found in him, because he was trustworthy."* — *Daniel 6:4*

The lions' den was merely the public reveal of a private posture. Daniel wasn't looking for a miracle; he was simply maintaining his alignment. Because the "yeast" of his character had been working in the dark for years, he was ready for the moment the world was finally watching.

But the story did not end there. The lions did not harm him, and by morning, he was found alive. Daniel's secret rhythm brought him divine protection. His story reminds us that private obedience often carries public impact.

Here are a few ways to work on obedience without an audience:

- **Choose Integrity in Secret** — Do what is right even when no one is watching. Keep promises quietly, without seeking recognition.
- **Practice Hidden Faithfulness** — Maintain private rhythms of prayer, service, or forgiveness that no one else sees. Let your obedience be consistent in the shadows.
- **Let Go of Validation** — Resist the urge to share every act of obedience. Release the need for applause or acknowledgement, and let your "Yes" be for God alone.
- **Embrace the Dark Corner of Preparation** — Stay faithful in unseen seasons, trusting that hidden growth is building strength for future responsibility.
- **Guard Integrity Over Image** — Choose honesty in private matters, even when they will never be audited or applauded. Integrity is the yeast that strengthens character.

- **Align with God's Rhythm** — Continue your obedience as Daniel did, keeping steady habits regardless of decrees, attention, or audience.

The Cost:

1. Letting go of the "hit" of recognition and the desire for immediate validation.
2. Choosing the "dark corner" of preparation instead of rushing toward the spotlight.
3. Remaining faithful even when the work feels overlooked or "invisible."

The Value:

1. An unshakable integrity that remains steady whether a crowd is watching or not.
2. A character that has been "strengthened from within," capable of sustaining great expansion.
3. A deep, sincere trust built through a private history with God that no one can take away.

Reflection:

1. Do you find it harder to stay faithful when no one notices?
2. Which habits in your life are shaped by integrity rather than recognition?
3. Would you continue your obedience if no one ever knew?

Today's Step:

1. Perform one act of obedience today entirely in secret. Whether it is a quiet service or a hidden sacrifice, let it stay in the "dark corner."
2. Do not share it on social media, do not tell a friend, and do not seek acknowledgement.
3. At the end of the day, notice the quiet strength that grows when your "Yes" is for God alone.

What you do in secret shapes what God reveals in public.

Day 12 - Obedience Without Immediate Reward

Obedience without immediate reward is the training ground for sustained capacity. Most people are fuelled by the high of a visible win, but true alignment is forged when you continue to labour while the profit is still invisible. This is not merely about waiting for a date on a calendar; it is about the stabilisation of your soul so it can eventually bear the weight of significant impact.

When the reward is deferred, God is decoupling your faithfulness from your feelings. He moves you from a performance-based posture, where you only act when you see a return, to a purpose-based one. This process ensures that your commitment is rooted in who He is, rather than what He is currently providing.

If the reward were the only fuel for your obedience, you would be unable to sustain the high-pressure responsibilities of the seasons to come. By practising faithfulness in the silence, you are building the internal structural integrity required to handle the abundance of the future without collapsing under its weight.

Imagine an old-school photographer developing a masterpiece. The photo has already been captured on film, but for that image to become permanent and visible, the film must be submerged in a series of chemical baths in near-total darkness.

During this stage, the paper appears blank. There is no shape, no colour, and no evidence of a reward for the work being done. If the photographer grows impatient and turns on the bright lights to "check" for a result too soon, the image is instantly scorched and destroyed.

The lack of an immediate image is not a failure in production; it is the chemical fixing required for a permanent finish.

Obedience without reward is the process of making your alignment light-proof. God is not withholding the result; He is ensuring that when the light of success finally hits you, the image of your character doesn't fade or dissolve under the heat of public pressure.

This darkroom phase is where your motives are purified, ensuring that you are doing the right thing because it is right, not because it is being noticed.

King David's life is a vivid demonstration of this chemical fixing. He was anointed as king while still a young shepherd boy, but he immediately returned to the silence of the fields.

He spent the next thirteen to fifteen years in caves and wilderness hideouts, unrewarded and often hunted by the very kingdom he was destined to lead.

During those years, his promise looked like a blank piece of paper. David had multiple opportunities to "force" his reward by taking King Saul's life and seizing the throne early. However, he refused to turn on the lights prematurely.

"Wait for the Lord; be strong and take heart and wait for the Lord." — Psalm 27:14

He understood that his true success was not the crown, but the unshakable weight-bearing character he was forging in obscurity.

The "nothing" that happened in the caves was actually the anchoring of a dynasty that would endure for generations. The wilderness was not a detour; it was the vat of chemicals that fixed his soul to be "a man after God's own heart."

David's greatest legacy is not found in his crown, but in the Book of Psalms, a spiritual journal forged across a lifetime of unrewarded obedience.

These sacred songs and prayers were born in the transition from shepherd boy to fugitive to king. The most profound entries weren't written on the throne, but in the "darkroom" of the wilderness. They prove that the waiting did not delay his purpose; it created the depth and capacity required to sustain it.

Today, those same writings serve as a guide for seekers, demonstrating that what is developed in the shadows is what eventually provides light for the world.

Here are a few ways to work on obedience without immediate reward:

- ***Continue Faithfulness When Profit Is Invisible:*** Keep following God's instructions even when no visible outcome appears. Treat the silence as part of the process, not a failure.
- ***Choose Purpose Over Performance:*** Act because it is right, not because it is noticed. Anchor your obedience in God's character rather than immediate results.
- ***Resist the Urge to Force Outcomes:*** Refuse shortcuts or premature actions that try to "turn on the lights" too soon. Trust that hidden seasons are fixing your soul for permanence.
- ***Practice Excellence in the Darkroom:*** Do your work with care, even when it feels unseen. Like a photographer in darkness, let the unseen stage prepare the image of your character.
- ***Anchor in God's Timing:*** Remind yourself daily: "The reward is not delayed; it is being prepared." Speak this truth when impatience rises.
- ***Celebrate Internal Capacity:*** Reflect on one way this hidden season is strengthening you—patience, endurance, humility—and thank God for the unseen growth.

The Cost:

1. Continuing to follow instructions when the profit is invisible.

2. Choosing faithfulness when your "promise" looks like a blank page.
3. Refusing to "force" a result before your soul is chemically fixed.

The Value:

1. Developing a soul that success and public scrutiny cannot scorch.
2. Building a foundation deep enough to sustain a legacy, not just a moment.
3. The integrity required to handle the abundance when it arrives.

Reflection:

1. If you knew the reward was ten years away, would you still be as faithful today?
2. Is your current frustration about a lack of progress, or simply a lack of proof?
3. How is this "blank paper" season fixing an image of God's character in you?

Today's Step:

1. Identify one responsibility you've thought about dropping because it seems to yield no profit.
2. Practice it today with intentional excellence, as if the reward were already visible.
3. At the end of the day, answer this: "If this hidden season is a fixing process, what specific internal capacity is it making permanent in me?"

Obedience pays in seasons, not moments.

Day 13 - Obedience Under Resistance

Obedience under resistance is the decision to remain steady when the pressure pushes back. When we hit an obstacle, our survival instinct usually offers two primal options: Fight or Flight.

We either lash out at the resistance in frustration or we retreat to the safety of the "runway" to avoid the friction. But in the architecture of growth, there is a third, higher option: ***The Climb***.

Think of a massive aircraft preparing for take-off. A plane does not rise by "fighting" the wind with raw aggression, nor does it "flee" from it. It rises by accelerating directly into the headwind. It is the very force screaming against the wings that creates the lift needed to leave the ground. Without that friction, the plane remains earthbound and trapped. What feels like opposition is not a signal to quit; it is the mechanical requirement for your elevation.

This is lived out at the Point of Friction, the exact moment where your conviction meets a counter-force.

Instead of Fight: Don't waste your energy arguing with critics or complaining about the difficulty. You stay focused, letting the "wind" of their noise provide the lift for your quiet excellence.

- ***Instead of Flight:*** You don't abandon the project because it got heavy. You realise the runway is for parking, but the sky is for a purpose.

Choosing the harder "Yes" when a "No" would be more comfortable is how you generate the velocity required to break the pull of the ordinary.

Every time you hold a boundary that invites disappointment, or choose honesty that costs you an easy exit, you are thinning the drag on your life. You aren't being stalled; you are achieving an altitude that those who avoid the wind will never reach.

Nehemiah, an exiled Israelite, served as a royal cupbearer in the Persian court. He was a mastermind in choosing 'The Climb' over 'Fight or Flight'.

When he began the work of rebuilding Jerusalem's walls, the effort was not welcomed by everyone. Critics mocked the work, doubting its success, while others levelled accusations of rebellion. As progress continued, threats escalated into planned attacks.

Nehemiah could have fled back to the luxury of the Persian palace. Instead, he integrated resistance into the mission. He organised the work with strategic precision, assigning families to rebuild sections directly facing their own homes.

To survive the threats, the builders adapted: they carried materials with one hand and kept protection nearby with the other. They built while they watched, and they watched while they built. Nehemiah reminded the people that God was with them. He also stressed that their work had purpose.

Despite opposition, distraction, and intimidation, Nehemiah refused to be grounded by the headwind. Hence, a project that had been delayed for a century was finished in a staggering 52 days. The resistance didn't break the mission; it proved the power behind it.

"Blessed is the one who perseveres under trial because, having stood the test, that person will receive the crown of life that the Lord has promised to those who love him." — James 1:12

The result was more than a rebuilt wall—it restored confidence and security among the people. Even their enemies recognised that the work had been accomplished with God's help.

Here are a few ways to work on obedience under resistance:

- ***Choose The Climb Over Fight or Flight:*** When pressure pushes back, don't lash out or retreat. Face the resistance directly, letting it generate the lift for your growth.
- ***Focus Instead of Fighting:*** Refuse to waste energy on critics or complaints. Channel the "wind" of opposition into quiet excellence and steady progress.

- ***Stay Present Instead of Fleeing:*** Resist the urge to abandon the task when it feels heavy. Remember: the runway is for parking, but the sky is for purpose.
- ***Turn Friction into Velocity:*** Use boundaries, honesty, and difficult choices as the drag that creates altitude. Each hard "Yes" thins the pull of the ordinary.
- ***Build While Guarding:*** Like Nehemiah's builders, keep working with one hand while staying alert with the other. Adapt to resistance without halting the mission.
- ***Anchor in God's Presence:*** Remind yourself that God is with you in the headwind. Speak His promise aloud when resistance rises, and let His strength steady your climb.

The Cost:

1. Staying steady when the applause stops, and the pressure starts.
2. Choosing to stay in the room when your mind is already halfway out the door. Committing to the process even when the "data" shows zero progress.

The Value:

1. Developing a grit that doesn't crack just because someone raised their voice.
2. Turning raw anxiety into functional strength. The quiet authority that only comes from not running away.

Reflection:

1. Where are you currently being "pushed," and is your first instinct to push back or to fold?
2. If this obstacle is actually a catalyst, what is it trying to "lift" in your character?
3. What is one thing you would do today if you weren't afraid of the friction?

Today's Step:

1. Name the one project or conversation you've been avoiding because it feels "too heavy."
2. Give it exactly five minutes of your best energy today.
3. Don't worry about finishing; worry about showing up in the face of the resistance.

Small steps taken under pressure still move you forward.

Day 14 - Obedience When Tired

Obedience does not require perfect energy or an ideal mood. There are seasons when faithfulness feels heavy, and even the simplest responsibility feels like a mountain. This fatigue isn't just physical; it's a saturation of the mind, emotions, and spirit.

Consider the life of a customer service representative in a high-volume call centre. A ten-hour shift. The next call pings the split second the previous one ends. Some voices are kind; others are frustrated; a few are openly harsh. Each issue must be de-escalated, understood, and resolved before the next voice arrives. There is no pause, no silence, and no time to reset.

Over hours of constant output, the mind begins to fray. You must remain emotionally steady even when your heart is depleted. Your voice must remain calm even when your throat aches. I know this rhythm intimately—I lived it for over a decade.

When the shift finally ends, you carry that weight home. The weekend becomes a desperate scramble for recovery—sleep, chores, and the looming shadow of Monday. True rest feels like a fleeting breath before the cycle restarts.

Even here, obedience has a home. It's found in choosing patience with one more person when you have nothing left to give. It's the decision to be gentle when irritation would be easier. It is the act of turning your heart toward God in the three seconds of silence between tasks. This isn't "dramatic" obedience; it is steady devotion in the trenches of ordinary fatigue. This is where God anchors the deepest endurance.

This tension between doing and being is not new. Even Jesus' inner circle felt the crushing pressure to perform. In the story of Mary and Martha, we see this play out. Martha was consumed by the "shift"—the preparation, the serving, the logistics. In her exhaustion, she became distracted and resentful. Mary, however, chose to sit.

"Martha, Martha," the Lord answered, "you are worried and upset about many things, but few things are needed—or indeed only one. Mary has chosen what is better, and it will not be taken away from her." — Luke 10:41–42

The lesson isn't that work is wrong, but that obedience includes the wisdom to pause. Faithfulness isn't a performance; it's a response to what God is asking of you right now. Sometimes, the most obedient thing you can do is admit you are at your limit.

Here are a few ways to work on obedience when tired:

- ***Choose Patience Over Irritation:*** When fatigue tempts you to snap, respond gently instead. Offer one calm word where frustration would be easier.

- ***Turn Small Pauses into Prayer:*** Use brief moments of silence between tasks to turn your heart toward God, even if only for three seconds.
- ***Serve Slowly Instead of Rushing:*** Take one ordinary responsibility today and do it with intentional slowness and gratitude, rather than pushing through on autopilot.
- ***Let God See Your Exhaustion:*** Admit your limits honestly in prayer. Obedience includes surrendering your weakness, not pretending to be strong.
- ***Choose Rest as Obedience:*** Like Mary, pause when your "Martha-tasks" overwhelm you. Sit in God's presence, even briefly, and let Him reset your spirit.
- **Celebrate Hidden Endurance:** Always reflect on one way you stayed faithful despite fatigue. Thank God for anchoring your endurance in ordinary moments.

The Cost:

1. Choosing grace when your patience has been officially "timed out."
2. Answering softly when your mind is screaming for silence.
3. Letting God see your genuine exhaustion instead of performing "strength."

The Value:

1. A faith that holds steady on boring, exhausting, ordinary days.
2. Resilience that grows in the hidden places where no one is cheering.

3. A heart that finally learns to lean because its own legs have given out.

Reflection:

1. When you are "running on empty," what is the first part of your character that starts to leak?
2. Is there a "Martha task" in your life that you need to put down so you can actually hear God's voice?
3. What does "obedient rest" look like for you today?

Today's Step:

1. Identify one small act of service or a habit you usually rush through.
2. Do it today with intentional slowness and quiet gratitude.
3. Once finished, allow yourself a window of rest—without the guilt of what isn't done.

God works with willing hearts, not perfect energy.

Day 15 - Obedience When Misunderstood

When you move in alignment with God, you are often following a map others cannot see. What feels like a clear directive in prayer may look like a chaotic detour from the outside. Because others aren't privy to the vision God has shared with you, they may mislabel your obedience as a mistake.

Being misunderstood does not mean you are wrong; sometimes it simply means your journey has details others are not meant to know. It takes maturity to stop seeking constant approval for what you have already settled with God.

Paul's ministry was a constant collision with public opinion. He spoke directly to this tension:

"Am I now trying to win the approval of human beings, or of God? Or am I trying to please people? If I were still trying to please people, I would not be a servant of Christ." — Galatians 1:10

Paul reminds us that loyalty to God and the pursuit of popularity rarely move in the same direction. If being liked becomes your primary goal, your conviction becomes negotiable. He understood that following Christ might set him against the crowd, but his identity was anchored in his role as a "servant" to one Master.

Think of a conductor leading an orchestra. The musicians are locked onto the conductor's baton, following a complex musical score that the audience never sees. When the conductor signals a sudden, jarring silence, the crowd might think the performance has failed. But that pause is a deliberate part of the composition.

The musicians aren't playing for the audience's immediate understanding; they are following the conductor's lead. In the same way, wisdom often looks slow or unsuccessful before the final movement is revealed.

Joseph's life was a definitive case study in being misread. His brothers misunderstood his dreams; Potiphar's wife misrepresented his character; the cupbearer forgot his help. He faced constant opportunities to defend himself, yet he chose to stay faithful in the silence.

In time, God positioned him where his integrity mattered more than his reputation. Eventually, the same people who once misunderstood him had to depend on his wisdom. His story proves that while obeying God may cost you approval now, it positions you exactly where you need to be later.

Here are a few ways to work on obedience when misunderstood:

- ***Choose Alignment Over Approval:*** Anchor your obedience in God's directive, not in people's opinions. Let His "Well done" outweigh the crowd's misunderstanding.

- ***Walk Quietly Instead of Defending:*** Resist the urge to overexplain or justify your choices. Offer excellence in action rather than explanations in words.
- ***Trust God with Your Reputation:*** Like Joseph, allow God to vindicate your integrity in time. Focus on faithfulness, not on proving yourself right.
- ***Follow the Conductor's Lead:*** Stay tuned to God's rhythm even when others misread the pauses or detours. Remember the score is His, not theirs.
- ***Release the Need to Be Liked:*** Accept that popularity and conviction rarely move in the same direction. Choose loyalty to Christ over universal approval.
- ***Celebrate Peace in Conviction:*** Reflect at the end of the day on the quiet peace that comes from obeying God, even when misunderstood. Thank Him for anchoring your identity in His truth.

The Cost:

1. Letting go of the desperate need to be "right" or fully understood by the crowd.
2. Accepting that people will misjudge your "slow" progress or quiet choices.
3. Trading the safety of universal approval for the depth of personal conviction.

The Value:

1. A life defined by your "score" with God rather than the noise of opinions.
2. A foundation that does not shift or shatter based on people's reactions.

3. The deep peace that grows when your identity is anchored in God's "Well done."

Reflection:

1. Whose approval is currently acting as a "volume knob" on your obedience?
2. Where are you wasting energy over-explaining a decision that God has already settled in your heart?
3. How would your obedience change today if you weren't trying to be understood?

Today's Step:

1. Think of one decision or direction God has placed on your heart that others have questioned.
2. Instead of defending it, commit to walking it out quietly and faithfully.
3. Offer excellence rather than an explanation.

If God called it, you don't need to explain it.

Day 16 - Obedience Beyond Appearance

Obedience is not validated by the metrics of public approval, but by the integrity of your private world.

It is entirely possible to maintain the mechanics of faith, attending the right gatherings, using the right vocabulary, and projecting a 'healed' aesthetic—while your internal life remains in a state of compromise. This isn't obedience; it is performative identity.

We live in an era that incentivises looks and appearance over heart and character. For many, especially those navigating a hyper-connected world, life has become a series of curated moments designed to secure social capital. We have become experts at managing our "vibe" while neglecting our values.

It is a frightening reality that we are often more concerned with how our life is perceived than how it is actually lived. This creates a dangerously thin line.

One can perform actions that look identical to obedience—advocating for justice, practising self-care, or sharing spiritual quotes—yet do them entirely to manufacture a specific image in the minds of others.

When the goal is to be seen as authentic rather than to actually be aligned, you aren't following God; you are chasing an algorithm. Real obedience is what remains when the phone is dead, the audience is gone, and there is no "like" button to validate your choices.

Jesus spoke directly to the high-functioning "influencers" of His day—the religious leaders who were obsessed with their public standing but hollow on the inside:

"These people honour me with their lips, but their hearts are far from me." — Matthew 15:8

God is never moved by a curated surface; He responds to the unfiltered soul.

Consider Judas Iscariot, whose journey serves as a definitive case study in divided loyalty. He was a part of the inner circle, he managed the finances, and looked like a leader to every observer. Yet, his proximity to the truth was not the same as his obedience to it.

His story is a stark reminder that you can be "trending" in a religious space while being completely disconnected from the heart of God.

Living for appearance is exhausting. It requires a constant awareness of how you are being perceived at all times. When your obedience is tied to your image, you are perpetually performing for an audience that is never satisfied. This is why so many are burnt out—not from doing too much, but from pretending too much.

Zero-Maintenance integrity is the ultimate goal. It is the psychological rest that comes when your private reality and your public image finally become the same person. You don't have to "keep your story straight" or remember which version of yourself you presented today, because your life is the story.

Here are a few ways to work on obedience beyond appearance:

- ***Choose Integrity Over Image:*** Let your private reality match your public words. Stop curating a "look" of obedience and focus on living it authentically before God.
- ***Stop the Need to Be Liked:*** Release the pressure to appear polished or successful. Allow honesty and humility to outweigh the pursuit of approval.
- ***Let God Audit Motives:*** Invite Him to examine your secret intentions, not just your visible actions. Pray for purity of heart rather than performance.
- ***Practice Zero-Maintenance Integrity:*** Align your inner life and outer life so they are the same person. Live in a way that requires no "story management."
- ***Reject Performative Faith:*** Resist the temptation to post, project, or perform obedience for social credit. Do good for an audience of One.
- ***Celebrate Freedom in Authenticity:*** Reflect at the end of the day on the peace that comes when you have nothing to hide, no image to defend, and no persona to maintain.

The Cost:

1. Overcome the need to be "liked" so you can finally be honest.
2. Accepting that true obedience might make you look "unsuccessful" or "unfiltered" to the world.
3. Allowing God to audit your secret motives, not just your public outputs.

The Value:

1. A character that doesn't fracture when the spotlight turns off.
2. The freedom of not having to remember which "version" of yourself you presented to the world today.
3. The peace of having nothing to hide and no "identity" to defend.

Reflection:

1. If you were prohibited from ever telling anyone about your "good deeds," would you still do them?
2. Are you more afraid of God seeing your flaws or the world seeing your "unpolished" reality?
3. Where is the gap between your "online persona" and your "offline character" the widest?

Today's Step:

1. Perform one act of "quiet obedience" that offers you absolutely no social credit.
2. Do not post it, do not mention it in conversation, and do not use it to "balance" your conscience.

3. Let it be a private transaction between you and God. Practice being good for an audience of one.

Real obedience is not about looking aligned — it is about being aligned.

Day 17 - Pause, Reflect and Reset

You have spent the last 16 days practising obedience in small, intentional ways. You've audited your desires, your timing, and your deepest motivations. You've looked into the darkroom of development and stood firm against the headwind of resistance. Now, you've arrived at the **Mirror.**

The Power of Pause:
Growth is not a product of constant motion; it is a byproduct of reflection. What you pause to consider, you begin to understand. What you understand, you can finally integrate. Today is not about striving or hitting a new metric. It is about noticing.

Obedience is not a race to be won; it is a relationship to be nurtured. Every healthy relationship requires moments of quiet recalibration. God rarely shouts over the noise of our hustle; He often speaks most clearly in the stillness.

You are not falling behind by resting; you are creating the necessary internal space to absorb what God is forming within you.

Your Mirror Moment

1. Where have you noticed a genuine shift in your heart over the last 16 days?
2. Which specific day triggered the most internal friction for you?

3. Which lesson has become a recurring "voice" in your daily decisions?
4. In which area has obedience transitioned from a chore to a natural rhythm?
5. Where does the "thin line" between appearance and alignment still feel the most difficult to navigate?

The Internal Audit

Write with unfiltered honesty about what this journey has revealed regarding:

1. Your Patterns: What is your go-to "exit strategy" when things get heavy?
2. Your Resistance: What are you still trying to protect from God's influence?
3. Your Progress: Where have you surprised yourself with your own resilience?
4. Your Relationship: How has your "view" of God changed as you've practised saying "Yes"?

Do not judge your data. Just notice it!

Today's Invitation:

1. Permit yourself to decelerate.

Pray. Reflect quietly. Rest intentionally.

The remaining days of this 33-day journey will build on the foundation laid here.

Sometimes obedience looks like a massive leap; today, obedience looks like sitting still. Both are essential for the climb ahead. Rest isn't falling behind—it's how you catch up with your soul.

Obedience pays in seasons, not moments.

PART IV — DEEP INNER ALIGNMENT

Day 18 - Waiting Without Anxiety

Waiting is not a void in your timeline; it is the environment where trust is structurally reinforced. For many, however, waiting isn't "quiet time"—it is a battlefield. Whether you are navigating a mind that never stops racing, a heart that feels perpetually on edge, or a spirit exhausted by heavy emotional shifts, anxiety isn't a lack of faith; it is a visceral response to a world that feels unsafe.

When your internal world is in a state of "high alert," the instruction to "just wait" can feel like an impossible demand. Anxiety grows when we try to carry what is not ours to control, especially when our minds struggle to distinguish between a "future possibility" and a "present threat." This makes it exhausting to look at tomorrow, let alone next year.

Responsible waiting in this context is not a demand for "perfect peace." It is the strategic decision to focus only on the next right step. It is trusting the Architect's Blueprint — the belief that even when you cannot see the finished structure, the physics of the build are still holding you. It is the realisation that God does not measure your surrender by your calmness, but by your willingness to stay in the process.

The Israelites at the Red Sea were experiencing a moment of pure, overwhelming panic. They had a physical barrier ahead and a terrifying past chasing them from behind. Their bodies were screaming for flight or fight. In that moment of visceral terror, Moses' directive was not a dismissal of their fear, but a boundary for it:

"Do not be afraid. Stand firm and you will see the deliverance the Lord will bring you today. The Egyptians you see today you will never see again. The Lord will fight for you; you need only to be still." — Exodus 14:13–14

Stillness in the middle of a mental storm does not mean "feeling good." It means not overreaching. It means acknowledging the terror without letting it dictate your direction.

The miracle followed the stillness—the quiet, gritty decision to stay put when every nerve told them to run. Deliverance arrived through a path they could never have engineered, proving that God is not waiting for your anxiety to vanish before He starts working.

Here are a few ways to work on waiting without anxiety:

- ***Release Worry:*** Stop treating anxiety as if it were productive. Recognise that worrying does not prepare you; it only drains you.
- ***Focus on the Next Right Step:*** Narrow your attention to what you can do in the next hour. Leave tomorrow in God's hands and act only on what is possible now.

- ***Shift From "What If?" to "What Is?":*** Replace anxious projections with present truth. Speak aloud: "God is here with me now."
- ***Stand Firm in Stillness:*** Like Israel at the Red Sea, resist the urge to run. Acknowledge the fear but refuse to let it dictate your direction.
- ***Trust the Great Architect's Blueprint:*** Believe that unseen progress is being built even when you cannot see the structure. Rest in the Designer's plan.
- ***Practice Short Pauses of Release:*** When distress rises, commit to 15 minutes of not solving the problem. Use that time to breathe, pray, and hand the weight back to God.

The Cost:

1. Releasing the exhausting idea that "worrying" is a productive form of "preparing."
2. Letting go of the need to solve "next month" when you only have the capacity for "right now."
3. Accepting that the most significant outcomes form in the "quiet" spaces you cannot see or influence.

The Value:

1. The relief of not having to perform "wellness" to be loved by God.
2. Developing a resilience that acknowledges the storm but isn't defined by it.
3. A deeper trust that allows you to be patient with your own limits.

Reflection:

1. If God isn't asking you to solve "tomorrow" today, what weight can you legally set down right now?
2. How can you shift from "What if?" (the fear of the unknown) to "What is?" (the truth of God's presence) in this moment?
3. For those supporting someone in a storm: How can you offer a "presence of peace" rather than a "pressure to change"?

Today's Step:

1. Identify one situation causing you distress. Instead of solving it, commit to simply not trying to solve it for the next 15 minutes.
2. Write down the one thing you can actually do in the next hour. Complete only that.
3. Visually, "place" the rest of the problem into the Architect's hands.

Peace is not the absence of the storm; it is the presence of the Great Architect.

Day 19 - Restraint Without Resentment

Choosing not to act on every impulse is a quiet form of inner strength. In a world designed to trigger an immediate "click," "post," or "purchase," the greatest test of your character isn't what you can achieve, but what you are willing to forgo for the sake of your peace.

Holding back outwardly is a matter of discipline; doing so without bitterness is a matter of maturity. Obedience is only fully formed when the heart remains soft, even while your actions stay measured. True control is not a forced, brittle silence—it is the steadfast stability of a trust that doesn't need to explain itself.

Think of a heavy vault door. Its strength doesn't come from being "stubborn" or "stuck"—it comes from its internal alignment. A vault is built to withstand immense pressure, but it only moves when the internal tumblers are perfectly positioned. If those tumblers are even a fraction of a millimetre out of place, the door stays sealed. It isn't a failure of the door; it is a protection of the treasure inside.

Restraint is the alignment of your heart. When you feel the modern "itch" to react—to fire back a snarky comment, to soothe stress with an impulsive buy, or to force a door open that God has clearly closed—you are feeling the weight of the world pressing against you.

Resentment grows when we try to force our way through before we are ready. Restraint without resentment is the quiet confidence that refuses to move until you are in sync with the Master's key.

Jesus navigated this "shortcut culture" in the wilderness. After forty days, His body was in a state of high-alert hunger. The temptation wasn't just about bread; it was about instant relief. He had the power to change His circumstances with a word, yet He refused to move out of alignment with the Father's timing just to satisfy a temporary urge.

When the shortcut was offered, Jesus answered from a place of unshakeable internal security:

> *"It is written: 'Man shall not live on bread alone, but on every word that comes from the mouth of God.'" — Matthew 4:4*

He didn't act from the pressure of His hunger, nor did He resent the boundary of the wilderness. He trusted that God's Word was the only nutrient worth turning the key for. His choice proved that restraint is not about being "denied"; it is about being secure.

You were not designed to be a simple wooden door that can be kicked in by a bad day or a stray comment. You are a masterpiece of God's design, and you require precise alignment to function at your best. When you choose restraint, you aren't just "stopping"—you are protecting the treasure of your soul.

Here are a few ways to work on restraint without resentment:

- ***Choose Alignment Over Impulse:*** Pause before reacting to pressure. View restraint not as denial but as protection of the treasure within your soul.
- ***Hold Back Without Bitterness:*** When you resist a shortcut or urge, keep your heart soft. Let restraint be rooted in trust, not resentment.
- ***Wait for the Master's Key:*** Like a vault door, move only when God aligns the tumblers. Pray for His timing instead of forcing your own.
- ***Resist Shortcuts to Relief:*** Refuse quick fixes that promise instant comfort but compromise long-term peace. Trust that God's Word is the only true sustenance.
- ***Anchor in God's Word Over Want:*** When hunger or pressure rises, answer with Scripture as Jesus did in the wilderness. Let truth steady your restraint.
- ***Celebrate Security Over Reaction:*** Reflect at the end of the day on one moment you held back. Thank God for the peace that came from choosing restraint without resentment.

The Cost:

1. Sacrificing the "high" of an immediate, unmeasured reaction.
2. The tension of holding your ground while your impulses scream for relief.
3. Relinquishing the need to have the last word or the quickest fix.

The Value:

1. A character that cannot be "hacked" or broken by temporary stress.
2. The relief of making decisions from a place of depth rather than panic.
3. A heart that is governed by the "Word" rather than the "Want."

Reflection:

1. In which area of your life does "The Pressure of Now" feel heaviest—your notifications, your finances, or your need to be right?
2. Are you "holding back" with a locked, angry heart (resentment) or a secure, aligned heart (restraint)?
3. What "shortcut to relief" is currently tempting you to move before your internal tumblers are aligned with God's word?

Today's Step:

1. Identify one situation where you feel the urge to react quickly today—whether it's a text, a purchase, or a frustration.
2. Instead of fighting it with sheer willpower, view the restraint as a security measure for your peace.
3. Pause for sixty seconds before you act, and pray: "Lord, align my heart so that I only move when You turn the key."

Restraint today protects tomorrow's peace.

Day 20 - Trust Without Certainty

Certainty is a comfort, but it has never been a requirement for obedience. We live in an era of "total information"—where we don't pick a restaurant without fifty photos of the food, and we don't start a journey without a GPS predicting our arrival time to the minute.

Whether you grew up manually tuning a box TV or now navigate life through a VR headset, the struggle is identical: the modern heart is addicted to the "preview." We want to see the destination before we put the car in gear.

Spiritual maturity, however, begins exactly where your "data" ends. We stay paralysed, waiting to obey until we have a 360-degree view of the outcome. We treat God like a digital map that must show us every turn before we leave the driveway. But faith is not about seeing the whole path; it is about the deep inner alignment of trusting the One who designed the terrain.

Think of the shift from a printed manual to a blank screen. For decades, we relied on physical guides—maps you could fold, landlines with static locations, and instructions printed in ink.

Today, we rely on dynamic, ever-changing interfaces. When the screen goes blank or the signal drops, our first instinct is panic. We feel we cannot move because we cannot see the next frame.

Trust is the ability to keep walking when the screen is dark. It is the realisation that your "structural integrity" isn't powered by the information on the display, but by the Architect behind the device.

You are already a practitioner of trust; you board planes without meeting the pilot and accept prescriptions without knowing the chemistry. Spiritual trust simply asks you to pivot that same confidence away from "visible proof" and toward God's unchanging character.

This tension is captured perfectly in the account of the disciples on the Sea of Galilee. They were caught in a visceral conflict between their "high-alert" anxiety and a presence that defied their logic. They were exhausted by heavy emotional shifts, much like the Israelites at the Red Sea in Day 18.

When they saw that Jesus was walking on the water, their bodies screamed for "fight or flight." They clung to the boat—the only physical technology they understood—as their only source of certainty.

While the other eleven gripped the wood of the ship, Peter did something counterintuitive. He didn't ask for the storm to stop; he asked for a directive. He understood that the boat, though familiar, was now a barrier to the miraculous.

"Lord, if it's you," Peter replied, "tell me to come to you on the water." 'Come,' he said. Then Peter got down out of the boat, walked on the water and came toward Jesus. — Matthew 14:28-29

Peter's step was the ultimate act of responsible waiting. He stopped trying to engineer a way back to the shore and focused only on the next right step. He trusted the 'Blueprint' over his own eyes. Faith did not settle the storm; it simply shifted his weight. He moved his reliance from the wood he could grip to the One who holds the universe together.

Here are a few ways to trust without certainty:

- ***Let Go of the Need for Previews:*** Stop waiting for a "high-definition" preview before moving. Trust God's directive even when the outcome isn't fully visible.
- ***Step Out of the Boat:*** Identify what feels safe but is holding you back. Like Peter, move from familiar security into faith-driven obedience.
- ***Replace Data with Dependence:*** Resist the urge to overanalyse or demand details. Shift your reliance from information to God's unchanging character.
- ***Walk When the Screen Is Dark:*** Keep moving forward even when you cannot see the next frame. Trust that the Architect is guiding the terrain beneath your feet.
- ***Anchor in the Caller's Voice:*** Train your ear to recognise God's voice above the storm. Let His word, not your circumstances, determine your next step.

- ***Celebrate Movement Over Certainty:*** Reflect at the end of the day on one area where you acted without full clarity. Thank God for meeting you in motion.

The Cost:

1. Letting go of the need to see the "Arrival Time" before you start.
2. Moving forward, when staying in the "boat" feels more logical.
3. Releasing the right to know "how" it all ends before you say "yes."

The Value:

1. A heart that remains steady even when your "screen of certainty" goes blank.
2. Developing an ear that recognises the Caller's voice over the storm's roar.
3. Moving from being a spectator of the impossible to walking on top of what once scared you.

Reflection:

1. Are you waiting for a "high-definition" preview before taking a step you already know is right?
2. In your life right now, what represents the "Boat"—the thing that feels safe but is actually keeping you from your next level of growth?
3. If God gave you a clear direction but withheld the specific details of "how" and "when," what would be the biggest barrier to your movement today?

Today's Step:

1. Identify one area where "not knowing" has paused your progress. Instead of searching for more "data," take one micro-step today.
2. Whether it's a phone call, a difficult conversation, or a firm decision, let movement replace your analysis.
3. As you move, pray: "Lord, I don't need the map; I only need Your voice. I am stepping out because you called."

Certainty keeps you in the boat. Trust puts you on the water.

Day 21 - Peace Without Outcomes

Real peace is not a byproduct of life going your way; it is the result of staying aligned even when it doesn't. We tie our calm to our results. When the outcome of life is good, we relax. When the plan fractures, our peace drops with it. We have become "outcome-addicts," measuring our spiritual health by our visible wins rather than our internal posture.

But Scripture points to a different kind of peace—one that isn't dictated by the scoreboard. It is a peace that exists in the practice, not just the prize. Peace built on outcomes rises and falls like a fluctuating market. Peace built on obedience is a steady foundation that remains after the storm has passed.

Think of someone following a prescribed medical treatment. They take the medication, adjust their lifestyle, and follow the specialist's instructions to the letter.

Healing is a biological process that they cannot force or see happening in real-time, but there is a profound peace in the practice. They cannot control how quickly their body responds, but they find calm in knowing they are aligned with the best possible plan. Their trust in the expert's guidance brings rest even before the "cure" is visible.

Life requires this same "practice over outcome" mentality. Whether you are a parent loving a rebellious child, a student studying for an uncertain future, or a professional choosing integrity over a shortcut, your role is the action, not the aftermath. Doing what is right doesn't always bring a quick reward, but it builds a heart that is no longer held hostage by circumstances.

Here are three men—Shadrach, Meshach, and Abednego—who faced a choice that would test anyone's resolve.

They were ordered by King Nebuchadnezzar to bow to a massive golden image or be thrown into a blazing furnace. They believed with all their hearts that God was able to save them, but they made it clear that their obedience was not a transaction.

They looked the most powerful king on earth in the eye and delivered a response that has echoed through generations:

"King Nebuchadnezzar, we do not need to defend ourselves before you in this matter.
If we are thrown into the blazing furnace, the God we serve is able to deliver us from it, and he will deliver us from Your Majesty's hand.
But even if he does not, we want you to know, Your Majesty, that we will not serve your gods or worship the image of gold you have set up." — Daniel 3:16-18

The king, in a rage, ordered the furnace to be heated seven times hotter than usual. They were bound and thrown into the heart of the fire, yet the flames had no power over them. When the king looked in, he was stunned to see four instead of three men, walking freely and unbound in the midst of the heat.

Finally, when they stepped out, the crowd was silenced by the impossible: their hair wasn't singed, their clothes weren't scorched, and there wasn't even the smell of smoke on them.

What was meant to destroy them left no trace. Their obedience didn't just protect their lives; it revealed God's power to everyone watching.

Their peace didn't start when the king called them out of the fire. It started with the settled decision to obey, no matter the result. This miracle followed a heart that was already at peace.

Here are a few ways to work on peace without outcomes:

- ***Choose Alignment Over Results:*** Anchor your peace in obedience, not in visible wins. Let your calm come from doing what is right, not from how things turn out.
- ***Practice Peace in the Process:*** Treat faithfulness like a prescribed plan. Rest in the practice itself, even when the "cure" or the answer isn't visible yet.

- ***Let Go of the Scoreboard:*** Refuse to measure your spiritual health by outcomes. Release the exhausting need to prove success through results.
- ***Declare "Even If" Obedience:*** Like Shadrach, Meshach, and Abednego, choose to obey even if the outcome doesn't change. Let conviction outweigh circumstance.
- ***Surrender the Steering Wheel:*** Hand over the "how" and "when" to God. Write down your concern and declare: "My role is the practice; the outcome is God's."
- ***Celebrate Steadiness Over Surges:*** Reflect at the end of the day on one area where you stayed calm despite uncertainty. Thank God for anchoring your peace in Him, not in results.

The Cost:

1. Releasing the exhausting need for guaranteed outcomes.
2. Letting go of the "steering wheel" of how things must end.
3. Refusing to measure your success by how things appear to others.

The Value:

1. An inner steadiness that remains even when the "cure" or the "answer" is delayed.
2. A sense of self-worth rooted in who you are, not what you've achieved.
3. Breaking the cycle of "highs" and "lows" tied to results.

Reflection:

1. When plans fall apart, how quickly does your peace leave the room with it?
2. Is there a specific result—a job, a relationship, or a health report—that is currently carrying too much weight in your heart?
3. Who would you become if your peace stopped taking orders from your problems and started taking them from your purpose?

Today's Step:

1. Identify one goal or situation that is currently causing you concern.
2. Write it down, and beneath it, write: "My role is the practice; the outcome is God's."
3. Throughout the day, when the "itch" to control the result returns, repeat this as a declaration of surrender.

Peace borrowed from an outcome is always one bad day away from disappearing. Peace anchored in the One is as permanent as the Source.

Day 22 - Letting Go of Comparison

Comparison is a quiet leak in the structure of your joy. The moment you begin measuring your life against someone else's timeline, you lose the vertical alignment required for your own direction. We don't drift off course because we lack guidance; we drift because we cannot stop looking sideways.

In today's world, comparison has become a high-speed downward spiral. It is no longer just about "keeping up with the neighbours"; it is a digital weight that breeds deep negativity and nagging insecurity. We scroll through the "highlight reels" of others and mistakenly conclude that we are "not enough" or that everyone else is somehow "better."

This constant mental scorekeeping doesn't just make us unhappy—it can lead to a dark fog of depression.

Imagine being trapped in a room where every wall is a mirror. No matter which way you turn, you are confronted with reflections—your own flaws magnified and the distorted shapes of people passing by. You cannot see the door because you are too busy checking your position against the glass. Comparison is that mirrored room. It creates a mental clutter that chokes out your focus and drains your energy.

When you obsess over someone else's milestones—their promotion, their marriage, their house—you are effectively trying to live in their reflection. Letting go of this habit is like smashing the mirrors. It declutters your mind, allowing you to finally focus on the "better things" at hand: the unique work God has placed in your own lane.

There is a significant difference between the habit of comparison and the need to vent. If someone compares you to another person—perhaps a parent or a boss using a peer as a yardstick—it creates a wound that needs processing. Venting about that unfair comparison once or twice is an understandable way to clear the nagging weight from your chest.

However, we must be careful not to let venting turn into a permanent residence of gossip or bitterness. As a listener, you have a vital role in this structure. You have the right to protect your own mental alignment by rejecting a conversation that has become unhelpful or toxic. You can, and should, offer a firm but polite "no" to information that serves only to pull others down.

A healthy listener knows when to offer a shoulder and when to close the door on a narrative that is going nowhere.

We know from the Bible that before Jesus ascended to heaven, He appeared several times to His disciples and performed miracles as a testament to His resurrection. One of the most intimate encounters occurred on the shore of Galilee.

After a miraculous catch of fish, Jesus pulled Peter aside for a restorative conversation. Having denied Jesus three times during the crucifixion, Peter was likely carrying a crushing weight of shame. In a beautiful act of grace, Jesus asked Peter, "Do you love me?" three times—once for every denial—effectively reinstating his identity and giving him a new command: "Feed my sheep."

However, immediately following this deep restoration, Jesus gave Peter a sobering glimpse of his future, hinting that his life would eventually end in martyrdom. It was in this moment of heavy revelation that Peter's focus faltered. Instead of letting his new assignment settle, he looked back at the disciple John, who was following them, and asked, "Lord, what about him?"

Peter was looking for a scorecard; he wanted to know if John's path would be easier or more prestigious than his own difficult road. Jesus addressed this sideways glance directly to Peter. His response was a sharp call back to Deep Inner Alignment:

"If I want him to remain alive until I return, what is that to you? You must follow me." — John 21:22

Jesus was telling Peter, "John's path is not your assignment. His reflection is not your reality." Once Peter stopped looking sideways, he became a steady leader who could finally move forward. He learned that focusing on his own walk didn't make him selfish; it made him available.

Here are a few ways to overcome comparison:

- ***Smash the Mirrors Over Sideways Glances:*** Stop measuring your life against someone else's highlight reel. Break free from the mental clutter of mirrored comparisons.
- ***Focus on Your Lane Over Their Milestones:*** Redirect energy from tracking others' progress to pursuing the unique assignment God has placed in front of you.
- ***Vent Once, Don't Dwell:*** Process unfair comparisons briefly if needed, but refuse to let venting become gossip or bitterness. Keep conversations healthy and forward-moving.
- ***Protect Your Mental Alignment as a Listener:*** When others compare or criticise you, politely redirect or step away. Guard your peace by refusing toxic narratives.
- ***Follow Jesus' "What Is That to You?" Directive:*** Like Peter, stop asking about someone else's path. Obey the call God gave you, even if another's journey looks different.
- ***Celebrate Gratitude Over Envy:*** When tempted to compare, pause and write down three unique blessings in your own journey. Let gratitude reset your perspective.

The Cost:

1. Letting go of the exhausting habit of measuring your "middle" against someone else's "highlight reel."

2. Releasing the need to understand why someone else's journey looks smoother than your own.
3. Learning to say "no" to gossip or unhelpful comparisons, even when they are offered as "concern."

The Value:

1. A mind that is finally quiet enough to hear your own specific instructions.
2. Happiness that isn't dependent on being "ahead" of anyone else.
3. The freedom of a heart that answers only to the Caller, not the crowd.

Reflection:

1. Whose "mirrored" progress has been quietly dictating your mood or leading you into a cycle of nagging negativity?
2. Are you currently "venting" to heal a wound, or have you allowed the conversation to turn into a permanent habit of comparison?
3. If Jesus gave you a clear "Follow Me" today but gave someone else a different path, would you be content with your assignment alone?

Today's Step:

1. Identify one platform or person that triggers your urge to compare. Commit to a "no-sideways-look" policy for the next 24 hours.

2. If you feel the urge to vent about someone else's success, stop and write down three things unique to your journey that you are grateful for.
3. Practice your right as a listener: If a conversation turns toward unhelpful comparison or gossip, politely redirect it or step away.

Comparison looks sideways. Obedience moves forward.

Day 23 - When Delay Is Protection

A delay is often misdiagnosed as an obstruction when, in reality, it is a sophisticated form of structural preservation. However, it is rarely a simple no.

In a world that prizes speed — instant messages, rapid promotions, immediate feedback — stillness feels like failure. We measure progress by visible movement and assume that a closed door is a verdict. Yet many pauses are not punishments; they are deliberate halts placed between you and harm you cannot yet perceive.

What looks like a hindered plan is often the meeting point of the visible and the invisible. A cancelled meeting, a postponed interview, a stalled project or a sudden illness can be the hinge that keeps you from walking into something dangerous or destructive. The pause is not always a detour; sometimes it is a shield.

When your plans slow, God is inviting you to move from passive waiting to active sensing. Waiting is a calendar habit; sensing is a spiritual skill. Deep inner alignment trains you to recognise the difference between a stop that needs force and a stop that needs attention. Learn to hear the quiet command: **"Stop for your safety"**.

Imagine you're at the checkout, about to pay for something important, and your card payment declines. It's inconvenient, embarrassing and badly timed. You feel exposed and frustrated.

Later, you discover the bank blocked the transaction because someone tried to use your card fraudulently. What looked like an obstacle was actually protection. The bank's interruption cost you a moment of ease but saved you from a much larger loss, that of your savings.

Interruptions work the same way. They disrupt your plan at the worst possible moment so you don't walk into the worst possible outcome. The frustration you feel is real; the purpose behind the pause often is too. Learn to treat the interruption like a fraud alert: an awkward, unwelcome block that is nonetheless guarding what matters most.

Scripture gives a clear example of this protection where a delay seemed like trouble, but in reality, it was mercy.

Balaam was a respected prophet whose reputation travelled ahead of him; when King Balak sought to curse Israel, Balaam set out convinced his path was open and his assignment certain. From his vantage point, everything looked straightforward: a road to ride, a task to complete, and a reward to gain.

As he travelled, however, his donkey stopped, turned aside and pressed against a wall. Three times the animal refused to move; three times Balaam grew angrier and struck it. To Balaam, the pauses were obstacles that delayed his mission. He could not see what the animal saw, and the donkey had seen what Balaam could not.

Only when God opened Balaam's eyes did the truth appear: an angel stood in the road with a drawn sword, blocking the path. Balaam bowed low and fell facedown. Then the angel asked:

> *"Why have you beaten your donkey these three times? I have come here to oppose you because your path is a reckless one before me." — Numbers 22:32*

The donkey's resistance was not stubbornness but protection. Had Balaam forced his way through, he would have walked into imminent danger.

This exposes two familiar failures: spiritual short-sightedness and ego-driven urgency. Balaam assumed that movement equalled rightness; the donkey's pause revealed that movement without sight can be ruinous.

Discernment arrived only when he surrendered his timetable, embraced the pause, and allowed his eyes to be opened.

Here are a few ways to understand if delay is protection:

- ***Release Timetable Control:*** Accept pauses without forcing movement. Trust that God's timing may be shielding you from unseen harm.
- ***Treat Interruptions as Alerts:*** View delays like a fraud alert: inconvenient but protective. Let frustration give way to gratitude for what is being preserved.

- ***Move From Waiting to Sensing:*** Shift from passive waiting to active discernment. Ask: "Is this a stop for safety?" before pushing forward.
- ***Resist Ego-Driven Urgency:*** Refuse to equate speed with success. Recognise that reckless movement can be more dangerous than stillness.
- ***Learn From Balaam's Pause:*** Remember the donkey's resistance was protection, not obstruction. Trust that unseen barriers may be God's mercy.
- ***Celebrate Redirection Over Delay:*** Reflect at the end of the day on one delay that saved or redirected you. Thank God for the shield hidden in the pause.

The Cost:

1. Releasing your preferred timing, even when it feels unbearable to wait.
2. Accepting interruptions without demanding quick explanations.
3. Trusting when progress slows, even if others seem to be racing ahead.

The Value:

1. Protection from unseen harm that could have derailed your future.
2. Redirection toward wiser paths that you would not have chosen on your own.
3. Trust strengthened through patience, shaping a soul that moves with wisdom instead of haste.

Reflection:

1. Where has a recent delay frustrated you?
2. Could a closed door be protecting you from something unseen?
3. How do you usually respond when plans are interrupted — with frustration or with faith?

Today's Step:

1. Recall one delay from your past that later proved helpful.
2. Write how it protected or redirected you.
3. Let that memory shape how you view current delays.

Some delays are detours. Others are shields. Wisdom grows when you learn the difference.

Day 24 - Choosing Obedience Over Ego

Our ego often disguises itself as self-respect, but many times it is simply self-protection. It wants to be right, recognised, and reassured. Obedience is different. It is less concerned with appearance and more concerned with alignment.

Ego asks: "How do I look?" Obedience asks: "What aligns with God's instruction?" That single question can redirect an entire moment. It shows up in many forms:

- The need to win every argument.
- The refusal to apologise.
- Defending yourself before listening.
- Rejecting feedback quickly.
- Wanting credit but avoiding responsibility.

Ego isn't always loud. Sometimes it is the quiet voice that says, "Don't lower yourself." But humility isn't lowering yourself — it's lowering your pride.

An apology is a clear example. It can feel like losing ground, yet it often restores trust faster than being "right." Strong leaders apologise quickly. They value peace more than ego and growth over image. Daily obedience over ego can look like:

- Admitting you were wrong.
- Listening instead of preparing a defence.
- Choosing peace instead of proving a point.

We see this tension clearly in Naaman's life. He was a respected commander, accustomed to honour and visible authority. When he contracted leprosy, he sought healing from the prophet Elisha. Naaman expected a dramatic display — a grand gesture that matched his status.

Instead, Elisha gave him a simple instruction: wash in the Jordan River seven times. Naaman's pride reacted before his faith did. Scripture records:

"But Naaman went away angry and said, 'I thought that he would surely come out to me and stand and call on the name of the Lord his God, wave his hand over the spot and cure me of my leprosy. Are not Abana and Pharpar, the rivers of Damascus, better than all the waters of Israel? Couldn't I wash in them and be cleansed?' So, he turned and went off in a rage." — 2 Kings 5:11–12

The instruction felt too simple. Too small. Beneath his status. His ego nearly cost him his healing. Only after listening to wise counsel did he humble himself and obey the instruction. Then his skin was restored.

The change did not come from the water. It came from his willingness to lower his pride.

Letting go of ego is important. Our ego fights against change because it wants to preserve comfort and control. It slows down growth by keeping you stuck in old patterns, and it puts stress on relationships by making every disagreement a battle for pride. A teachable heart can be guided into new wisdom, but a defensive heart resists correction and remains closed.

Humility doesn't make you weak; it makes you reachable. It opens the door for wisdom to enter and for growth to take root. When you choose humility over ego, you become easier to guide, quicker to heal, and more ready for change.

Ego builds walls; humility builds bridges. Ego demands recognition; obedience seeks alignment.

The truth is simple: ego may protect your image for a moment, but humility protects your future for a lifetime.

Here are a few ways to overcome ego:

- ***Alignment Over Appearance:*** Shift the question from "How do I look?" to "What aligns with God's instruction?" Let obedience, not image, guide your response.
- ***Apologise Quickly Instead of Defending:*** Value peace over pride. Admit wrong without excuses, explanations, or softening. Humility restores trust faster than being "right."
- ***Listen Before Reacting:*** Resist the urge to prepare a defence. Hear feedback fully, even when it challenges your comfort or reputation.
- ***Choose Peace Over Winning:*** Let go of the need to win every argument. Prioritise reconciliation and growth over proving a point.

- ***Accept Simple Instructions Over Status:*** Like Naaman, obey even when the directive feels beneath your expectations. Healing often comes through humility, not grandeur.
- ***Celebrate Growth Over Image:*** Reflect at the end of the day on one moment where humility opened a door for wisdom or restoration. Thank God for the shift that obedience brought.

The Cost:

1. Releasing the need to look right, even when your reputation feels at stake.
2. Letting go of defensiveness and the instinct to protect your image.
3. Accepting simple or humble instructions that feel beneath your status or expectations.

The Value:

1. Restoration where pride once blocked progress — healing, clarity, or a breakthrough that ego would have delayed.
2. Stronger relationships that are built on humility, honesty, and trust.
3. Personal growth that ego would have slowed, as obedience opens the door to wisdom and change.

Reflection:

1. Where does pride make it hard for you to admit wrong?
2. Is there a simple step you resist because it feels beneath you?

3. What might change if you asked, "What aligns with God's instruction?" before reacting?

Today's Step:

1. Apologise sincerely where needed.
2. Don't explain, defend, or soften it. Just own it.
3. Notice the shift inside you when ego steps aside.

Obedience keeps you aligned with God's path; ego keeps you chasing your own.

Day 25 - Obedience Under Authority: Trusting God in Leadership

Obedience to God often shows up in how we respond to authority. Not all authority feels fair, wise, or easy to follow. Yet Scripture consistently connects respect for authority with trust in God's order. Authority does not replace God; it reflects the order He permits for stability. Learning to respond with wisdom and respect develops humility and self-control.

This does not mean agreeing with everything or supporting wrongdoing. Biblical obedience never asks you to sin. It does not tolerate abuse, injustice, or manipulation. Godly submission is not blind compliance; it is a posture of discernment that seeks His will above human agendas.

Wisdom and discernment are essential in obedience under authority. They help you recognise when honour is required, even in disagreement. Responding with respect does not mean silence in the face of wrong, but it does mean choosing humility over hostility. Honour in disagreement reflects trust that God remains sovereign over human systems. Scripture teaches:

> *"Let everyone be subject to the governing authorities, for there is no authority except that which God has established." — Romans 13:1*

Joseph served faithfully under leaders who misunderstood him. Daniel worked under kings who did not share his faith. Jesus Himself honoured earthly authority while remaining fully aligned with the Father.

Jesus recognised earthly authority but clarified its true source. When speaking to Pilate, He said:

"You would have no power over me if it were not given to you from above." — John 19:11

Jesus did not deny Pilate's authority, but He revealed its origin. All human authority operates under God's sovereignty. This perspective allows obedience to be rooted not in fear of people, but in trust in God.

Trusting God through authority shapes patience. It teaches us to slow down our instinct to react and instead to trust that God is working through structures we may not fully understand. Patience here is not passive waiting; it is active restraint. It is the discipline of holding back when emotions want to rush forward.

When you choose to honour authority even when you disagree, you are training your heart to resist impulsive reactions and to wait for God's timing. This kind of patience builds resilience, reminding you that not every battle needs to be fought immediately, and not every injustice needs to be corrected by your hand alone.

It also trains the heart to surrender control and trust God's oversight. Human authority often reminds us that we are not the final decision-makers. That can feel uncomfortable, especially when authority seems flawed or unfair. Yet surrendering control is an act of faith — it acknowledges that God sees what you cannot, and that He can work through imperfect systems to accomplish His purposes.

Sometimes God uses authority to refine character. A boss who challenges your ideas, a parent who sets boundaries, or a civic leader whose decisions frustrate you — each can become a tool God uses to shape humility and strengthen discipline. Authority can be a mirror that exposes pride, impatience, or defensiveness in us.

Resisting authority often reveals ego; submitting with discernment develops maturity. Over time, obedience under authority grows wisdom, because it teaches you to see beyond the immediate moment and to trust God's larger plan. What feels like restraint today may become the very lesson that equips you for greater responsibility tomorrow.

Here are a few ways to work on obedience under authority:

- ***Respect Authority While Trusting God:*** Honour leaders even when you disagree, remembering that all authority operates under God's sovereignty.
- ***Choose Humility Over Hostility:*** Respond with respect instead of defensiveness. Honour in

disagreement reflects maturity and trust in God's oversight.

- ***Practice Discernment Over Blind Compliance:*** Obey authority without tolerating sin or abuse. Seek God's will above human agendas.
- ***Anchor in God's Sovereignty Over Human Systems:*** Like Jesus before Pilate, recognise that authority is permitted by God. Let this perspective steady your posture.
- ***Allow Authority to Refine Character:*** Accept challenges from bosses, parents, or civic leaders as opportunities to grow humility, patience, and discipline.
- ***Celebrate Peace Over Control:*** Reflect at the end of the day on one area where you surrendered control to God through respecting authority. Thank Him for the peace that followed.

The Cost:

1. Surrendering the need to always be right.
2. Showing respect when emotions resist.
3. Trusting God's justice over personal reaction.

The Value:

1. Emotional maturity that strengthens your character.
2. Favour and credibility that open doors of influence.
3. Peace in situations you cannot control, rooted in God's sovereignty.

Reflection:

1. How do you respond when authority challenges your preference?
2. Do you show respect even when you disagree?
3. Where might God be shaping humility through authority in your life?

Today's Step:

1. Choose one authority figure in your life — workplace, family, civic, or spiritual.
2. Pray for them today.
3. Ask God to give you a respectful and wise posture in your interactions.

To obey authority is to trust that God is in charge, even when leaders make mistakes.

PART V — STEWARDSHIP, IMPACT & MULTIPLICATION

Day 26 - Obedience in Seasons of Abundance

Obedience is often tested more by abundance than by lack. In seasons of scarcity, dependence on God feels natural because our need is obvious.

We pray with urgency, cling to His promises, and recognise that without Him we cannot move forward. But when prayers are answered, doors open, and comfort arrives, the test changes.

Abundance can quietly shift our posture from dependence to self-reliance. Success, wealth, or stability can create the illusion of security, turning gratitude into entitlement and devotion into casual faith. True obedience in abundance means remembering that prosperity is a gift, not a substitute for God.

It is easy to enjoy blessings and forget the Source. Success, wealth, or stability can create the illusion that we are secure in our own strength. Gratitude fades into entitlement, and devotion becomes casual. True obedience in abundance means remembering that prosperity is a gift, not a replacement for God. It is the discipline of staying close to Him even when life feels full.

Obedience during times of plenty means guarding your heart. It requires recognising that answered prayers are not the finish line but the beginning of stewardship. Abundance is not meant to loosen your grip on God but to deepen it. Comfort whispers that you no longer need to pray as much, worship as deeply, or seek as earnestly. Yet obedience calls you to resist that drift and remain anchored.

Many people seek God intensely in need but grow casual in success. When life improves, alignment often decreases. But abundance is not meant to dilute devotion; it is meant to strengthen it. Prosperity should magnify dependence, not minimise it. The challenge is subtle — success can make us forget that we are still fragile without God's guidance.

Blessings are safest in the hands of those who remember where they came from. When gratitude remains alive, abundance becomes a tool for impact rather than a trap for pride. Remembering the Source keeps blessings in their proper place, preventing them from becoming idols. Prosperity is safest when it is stewarded with humility and obedience.

The true test of alignment is not how faithfully you cling to God in lack, but how steadfastly you walk with Him in abundance. Obedience in plenty proves whether your devotion is conditional or constant. It reveals whether blessings deepen your faith or distract you from it. Abundance is not dangerous in itself — it becomes dangerous only when it blinds us to the Giver.

Solomon's life shows this clearly. He was not David's oldest son or the obvious heir, yet God chose him to succeed David as king of Israel. Before David died, he publicly declared Solomon as the next king and instructed him:

"Walk in obedience to him, and keep his decrees and commands…" — 1 Kings 2:3

Solomon's leadership was meant to be rooted in obedience, not just authority. His reign began in a politically sensitive time, with rival claims to the throne. From the beginning, Solomon knew he needed God. When God appeared to him in a dream and said:

"Ask for whatever you want me to give you." — 1 Kings 3:5

Solomon asked not for wealth or victory, but for wisdom to govern well. This humility pleased God, who gave him wisdom along with wealth, honour, and influence.

His reputation spread far beyond Israel, and leaders from distant nations travelled to hear his counsel. Solomon came to be known as the wisest king of his time, and his influence reached across borders. The Temple he built in Jerusalem became a defining spiritual milestone, anchoring Israel's worship and standing as a visible testimony of God's favour.

His early reign was marked by humility, dependence on God, and a sincere desire to lead well — a posture that made his blessings safe in his hands. But his downfall, however, was gradual, not sudden.

As his power and wealth increased, so did his political alliances. Many alliances involved marriages to foreign women from countries with different gods. Over time, his heart became divided. He tolerated idol worship and even built altars for other gods to please his wives.

The problem was not marriage itself but compromise. Solomon did not reject God outright; he drifted from full alignment. Partial obedience slowly became disobedience.

His later thoughts in Ecclesiastes show a man who saw the emptiness of success without God. Wealth, pleasure, and achievement did not satisfy when alignment was lost. His conclusion was simple and weighty:

"Fear God and keep his commandments, for this is the duty of all mankind." — Ecclesiastes 12:13

Solomon's life shows that wisdom does not replace obedience. Blessing does not secure alignment. A strong start does not guarantee a steady finish. Abundance does not remove the need for obedience; it increases the responsibility for it. Alignment must remain constant, not conditional.

The true test of alignment isn't what you do with nothing. It's who you become when you have everything.

Here are a few ways to work on obedience in seasons of abundance:

- ***Guard Your Heart in Comfort:*** Stay alert when life feels full. Resist the drift of casual faith and keep gratitude alive.
- ***Choose Devotion Over Distraction:*** When success tempts you to relax spiritually, deepen your prayer, worship, and dependence on God.
- ***Practice Stewardship Over Self-Reliance:*** Treat answered prayers as the beginning of responsibility, not the finish line. Use abundance to serve, not to drift.
- ***Say No to Subtle Compromises:*** Refuse small concessions that erode devotion. Protect alignment even when compromise looks harmless.
- ***Anchor Blessings to the Source:*** Remember, prosperity is a gift, not a replacement for God. Keep Him central so abundance strengthens rather than weakens faith.
- ***Celebrate Humility in Success:*** Reflect at the end of the day on one blessing that drew you closer to God. Thank Him for provision and ask Him to keep your heart aligned.

The Cost:

1. Guarding your heart when life is comfortable, resisting the drift of casual faith.
2. Saying no to subtle compromises that seem harmless but erode devotion.

3. Choosing devotion over distraction when success tempts you to relax spiritually.

The Value:
1. Blessings that do not pull you away from God but deepen your dependence on Him.
2. Stability in success, where abundance strengthens rather than weakens your faith.
3. A life anchored to the Source, able to enjoy prosperity without losing alignment.

Reflection:
1. Has any blessing made you less dependent on God?
2. Where might comfort be softening your obedience?
3. Do you seek God as much in abundance as in need?

Today's Step:
1. Thank God specifically for three areas of provision in your life.
2. Then ask Him to keep your heart aligned as those areas grow.
3. Choose one small act of devotion today — prayer, generosity, or service — that reminds you He is the Source.

Blessings are gifts. Alignment keeps them in their proper place.

Day 27 - Obedience That Serves in Silence

We now shift from inward formation to outward impact.

Obedience does not stay hidden in your heart — it shows up in how you live for others. Some of the most powerful obedience is almost invisible. It simply answers the need. Legacy is rarely built on a stage. More often, it grows in ordinary moments where you choose to help when you could have walked away.

Quiet obedience is service without an audience. Picture yourself stopping to help someone with a flat tyre on a busy road. No photo. No post. No announcement. Just help. They may never know your name. Others may pass by without noticing. But for the one stranded, your choice changes their day. That is quiet obedience: not performance, but presence. Not recognition, but responsibility.

This same obedience includes giving to the less fortunate, not as a display, but as remembrance. Many forget that they once needed the same kindness they now have the power to give. Compassion grows deeper when you remember your own seasons of need.

Sometimes obedience looks like sharing a meal or paying for someone's essentials. Sometimes it means supporting quietly, so another person can breathe again. What God places in your hands is not only provision for you, but responsibility through you.

Jesus illustrated this in the story of the Good Samaritan. A man was beaten, robbed, and left on the roadside. Several people saw him and kept going. Then a Samaritan, from a group often looked down on, stopped. He treated the wounds, lifted the man onto his own animal, and paid for his care.

"But a Samaritan, as he travelled, came where the man was; and when he saw him, he took pity on him." — Luke 10:33

No applause followed. No crowd gathered. He simply saw a need and responded. His obedience looked like compassion in action. The outcome was not measured in recognition but in restoration. One man's life was changed because someone chose to act quietly. That is the hidden power of silent obedience — it creates impact without demanding attention.

Serving quietly does not make obedience small. It often makes it stronger, because sincerity is revealed when no one is watching. The absence of applause strips away performance, leaving only genuine compassion. Quiet alignment builds trust in unseen ways, reminding us that God values faithfulness over fame. Jesus Himself affirmed this principle when He said:

"Truly I tell you, whatever you did for one of the least of these brothers and sisters of mine, you did for me."
— Matthew 25:40

This means every unseen act of kindness is seen by God as service to Christ Himself. Helping the overlooked, the vulnerable, or those who cannot repay you is not wasted — it is worship. Quiet obedience honours God directly, even when no one else notices.

You are not called to be impressive. You are called to be faithful. Faithfulness in silence often plants a seed that grows beyond your sight. A simple act of kindness may ripple into generations, shaping lives you will never meet. The outcome of silent obedience is a lasting impact — unseen by crowds, but fully seen by God.

Here are a few ways to work on obedience, which serves in silence:

- ***Choose Presence Over Performance:*** Help quietly without seeking recognition. Let compassion guide your actions, not applause.
- ***Serve Without Announcement:*** Meet needs without posting, sharing, or reporting. Keep the service between you and God.
- ***Practice Compassion Over Credit:*** Give generously to those who cannot repay. Remember your own seasons of need and let gratitude fuel kindness.
- ***See Christ in "the Least":*** Treat every unseen act of service as worship. Recall Jesus' words: serving the overlooked is serving Him.
- ***Anchor Faithfulness in Silence:*** Resist the urge to make obedience visible. Let sincerity be revealed when no one is watching.

- ***Celebrate Hidden Impact:*** Reflect at the end of the day on one quiet act of kindness. Thank God for the unseen ripple it may create.

The Cost:

1. Letting go of recognition — serving "the least" even when no one applauds.
2. Serving without being noticed — choosing compassion when it will never be reported or remembered by people.
3. Giving when there is no return — helping those who cannot repay, trusting that God sees.

The Value:

1. A heart shaped by compassion — learning to see Christ in "the least."
2. Impact that reaches farther than you see — your quiet obedience may change a life in ways you'll never know.
3. Faithfulness that honours God — every hidden act becomes worship, because Jesus counts it as service to Him.

Reflection:

1. When are you most tempted to serve only when it is visible?
2. Is it harder to help when there is nothing in it for you?
3. How might Jesus be inviting you to serve "the least" in your daily life?

Today's Step:

1. Do one helpful act for someone who cannot repay you.
2. Do it quietly. Do not mention it. Do not post it. Let it remain between you and God.
3. Remember Jesus' words, serving "the least" is serving Him, and every hidden act of kindness is seen by heaven.

Quiet obedience rarely makes headlines, but it always makes a difference.

Day 28 - Ripple Effects of Obedience

A ripple effect occurs when a small action leads to a series of larger reactions. Drop a stone into water, and the surface doesn't just move once; circles keep spreading outward. The first action looks small, but its influence travels far beyond where it began. Long after the splash is over, the water is still moving.

Life works like that, too. Some actions don't end where they start. They travel into other people's lives, other moments, and sometimes other generations. A quiet decision to do what is right can reach further than a loud decision to be noticed.

Many people don't realise how much a single aligned step can achieve. It might be a word of honesty when silence feels easier, a refusal to join in when compromise seems normal, or a leap of faith when fear is loud.

These moments rarely feel historic, but they quietly shape history.

- One decision can change the direction of a family.
- One act of courage can open safety for others.
- One "yes" can interrupt a harmful pattern.

You may not see the full reach of your actions, but that does not make them small.

Rahab's story shows this clearly. She lived in Jericho, a city about to fall. She had heard of Israel's God and believed He was real. When Israelite spies entered the city, she faced a choice: protect herself or protect them. She chose to align with the God she believed in, even though it carried risk.

"By faith Rahab, because she welcomed the spies, was not killed with those who were disobedient." — *Hebrews 11:31*

Her decision did more than spare her life. It protected her family. And her story did not end there — she became part of the lineage of Jesus.

What looked like one risky choice in a single moment became a turning point that shaped generations.

- One choice.
- One moment.
- A ripple into history.

Rahab never saw how far her decision would travel. She could not have imagined that her act of faith would place her in the genealogy of Christ, or that her name would be remembered thousands of years later as an example of courage and obedience.

What seemed small in her lifetime became monumental in God's story.

The same can be true for you. Your responses shape outcomes you will never personally witness. A word of encouragement today might inspire someone to persevere years from now. A refusal to compromise could protect your family's integrity for generations. A single act of generosity might ripple into a legacy of kindness that outlives you.

Faithful surrender often feels ordinary in the moment, but its impact is extraordinary over time. You may never see the full reach of your choices, but heaven does.

God multiplies faithfulness in ways that extend beyond your lifetime, weaving your decisions into a story bigger than you can imagine.

Here are a few ways to create the ripple effects of obedience:

- ***Choose Alignment Over Ease:*** Do what is right even when blending in feels simpler. Let faithfulness interrupt harmful patterns.
- ***Stand Apart from Compromise:*** Refuse to join in when others accept shortcuts or dishonesty. Your "No" can protect more than just you.
- ***Practice Courage in Small Steps:*** Take one leap of faith when fear is loud. Remember that ordinary obedience often shapes extraordinary outcomes.
- ***Trust God Beyond Immediate Comfort:*** Obey even when clarity is missing. Believe that unseen ripples are forming through your surrender.

- ***Anchor in Rahab's Example:*** Recall her single act of faith that spared her family and placed her in Christ's lineage. Let her story remind you that one choice can echo for generations.
- ***Celebrate Hidden Influence:*** Reflect at the end of the day on one decision that may ripple forward. Thank God for multiplying faithfulness beyond what you can see.

The Cost:

1. Choosing what is right when blending in would be easier.
2. Standing apart from patterns others accept.
3. Trusting God beyond immediate comfort or clarity.

The Value:

1. Influence that outlives the moment and echoes into others' lives.
2. Protection that reaches beyond you, covering those connected to you.
3. A legacy shaped by steady faithfulness, even in small steps.

Reflection:

1. Who could be affected by your choices today without you realising it?
2. What pattern might your decisions interrupt or heal?
3. If your actions echoed forward, what would they repeat?

Today's Step:

1. Make one intentional choice today that aligns with God's instruction — even if it feels small.
2. Do it with faith, not fear.
3. Remember the ripple of that decision daily.

The step you take with God today may become the path someone else walks tomorrow.

Day 29 - Obedience in Leadership

Leadership is not confined to titles or positions. It shows up in everyday life — a parent guiding children, a friend offering wise counsel, a colleague stepping up when others hesitate, or someone choosing honesty over shortcuts.

Leadership is influence, and influence begins with alignment with what is right. Leadership is not about privilege; it is about responsibility.

True leadership starts with surrender to God's direction before asking anyone else to move. Authority grows where responsibility is accepted first.

Picture a lead bird in a V-formation. It isn't more important — it simply faces the headwind first. It absorbs resistance, so those behind can fly more steadily. In the same way, a leader often carries the discomfort of doing what is right first so others can move with clarity. Leadership is about going first, not being above.

Deborah's life shows this in action. She was both a judge and a prophet in Israel during a time of oppression. People sought her out because they trusted her discernment. She did not chase influence — she stewarded it.

God told Deborah to summon Barak, a military leader, during Israel's oppression. When the moment came, Deborah said:

> *"Go! This is the day the Lord has given Sisera into your hands. Has not the Lord gone ahead of you?" — Judges 4:14*

Barak hesitated. He agreed to go only if Deborah went with him. She consented, but told him the honour of victory would not be his because of his reluctance.

Then Barak went down Mount Tabor with ten thousand men following him. Instruction became action. Action became momentum. The victory that followed was not just military success. It came from leadership that listened first, then moved.

Deborah led by hearing. Barak led by acting. The people followed because they saw direction, not ambition.

Steps Toward Better Leadership:

1. Lead Yourself First — Obedience begins with personal alignment. Before guiding others, ensure your own choices reflect integrity, humility, and faithfulness.
2. Go First in Responsibility — Be the first to take responsibility, admit mistakes, and act on conviction. This builds trust and sets the tone for others.
3. Serve, Don't Control — Influence multiplies when people feel valued, not managed. Leadership is stewardship, not ownership.

4. Model Consistency — People follow what they see more than what they hear. Consistency in values and actions creates stability.
5. Listen Before You Lead — Deborah's leadership began with hearing God's voice. Leaders must listen to God, to wise counsel, and to those they serve.
6. Create Ripple Effects of Courage — Every act of obedience ripples outward. A leader's courage inspires others; compromise weakens the group.
7. Stay Humble in Success — Abundance and influence can tempt leaders to drift into pride. Guard your heart by remembering the Source.
8. Prepare for Legacy, Not Applause — Leadership is about long-term impact, not short-term recognition. Think generationally: your obedience today may shape tomorrow's culture.

Changing Leadership Styles for the Better:

Many leaders drift into patterns of control, pride, or performance. However, obedience in leadership calls for humility, listening, and alignment.

- Shift from control to stewardship — influence is not about owning people, but serving them.
- Shift from pride to humility — leadership is not about being seen, but about seeing others.
- Shift from performance to obedience — leadership is not about applause, but about alignment with God's direction.

When leaders lead with obedience, the ripple effect is profound. People stay when leadership is trustworthy; they leave when leadership is self-serving. The culture of a family, workplace, or community often reflects the posture of its leaders.

The Ripple Effect of Leadership:
Leadership decisions ripple outward. A leader's obedience can create safety, trust, and momentum for others. A leader's disobedience can create confusion, fear, and division.

- A parent's quiet obedience can shape a child's lifelong values.
- A manager's integrity can protect a workplace culture from compromise.
- A community leader's courage can inspire generations to stand firm in faith.

Whether you lead now or aspire to lead someday, remember: your choices will ripple into lives you may never meet.

For Current Leaders: Staying Grounded:
Leadership is not static; it requires continual alignment. Even seasoned leaders can drift into patterns of pride, control, or performance. Staying grounded means regularly returning to obedience, humility, and service.

- Re-examine your leadership style — ask if it is built on ambition or obedience, pride or humility, control or stewardship.

- Reset with obedience — when leadership feels heavy or unclear, return to God's direction. Alignment restores clarity.
- Remember the ripple effect — your choices shape culture. People stay under trustworthy leadership and leave when it becomes self-serving.
- Guard against complacency — influence can tempt leaders to coast. Stay sharp by listening, serving, and modelling consistency.
- Lead for legacy, not applause — measure success by the impact on people's lives, not by recognition or numbers.

For Aspiring Leaders: Staying Aligned:

If you are on the path to becoming a leader, remember:

- Integrity precedes influence. Who you are in private will shape how you lead in public.
- Obedience precedes opportunity. Aligning with God now prepares you for responsibility later.
- Faithfulness precedes fruitfulness. Small acts of obedience today ripple into a larger impact tomorrow.

5 Pillars of Obedient Leadership:

1. Integrity Before Influence — who you are in private shapes credibility in public.
2. Responsibility Before Authority — true authority grows where responsibility is carried first.
3. Service Before Control — leadership is stewardship, not ownership.

4. Listening Before Leading — discernment comes from hearing God and others before acting.
5. Legacy Before Applause — leadership is about long-term impact, not short-term recognition.

Here are a few ways to work on obedience as a leader:

- ***Lead Yourself First:*** Align your own choices with integrity and faithfulness before guiding others. Personal obedience builds credibility.
- ***Go First in Responsibility:*** Step into the headwind like the lead bird. Absorb resistance by acting on conviction, not comfort, so others can move with clarity.
- ***Serve, Don't Control:*** Treat leadership as stewardship. Value people over position and influence over ownership.
- ***Model Consistency:*** Live what you teach. Let your actions reflect your words so others see stability in your example.
- ***Listen Before You Lead:*** Hear God's voice, wise counsel, and those you serve. Like Deborah, discernment precedes direction.
- ***Create Ripple Effects of Courage:*** Let your obedience inspire others. One act of faith can multiply into collective momentum.
- ***Stay Humble in Success:*** Guard yourself against pride when influence grows. Remember the Source and keep your heart aligned.

- ***Prepare for Legacy, Not Applause:*** Lead with long-term impact in mind. Measure success by the lives shaped, not the recognition gained.

The Cost:

1. Going first when others hesitate — absorbing resistance so others can move forward.
2. Acting on conviction, not comfort — choosing obedience even when it feels costly.
3. Carrying responsibility, not just opinions — owning the weight of decisions instead of criticising from the sidelines.

The Value:

1. Influence that grows from integrity — people trust leaders who live what they ask of others.
2. Trust built through example — followers gain courage when they see obedience lived out.
3. Direction that helps others move forward — clarity comes when someone steps first into obedience.

Reflection:

1. Where do others quietly watch your example — at home, at work, or among friends?
2. Are you waiting for a title before you lead, or are you willing to lead through obedience now?
3. What step could you take first instead of waiting for someone else to move?

Today's Step:

1. Choose one area today where you can go first in doing what is right — whether at home, work, or in your community.
2. Act with conviction, not comfort — start the task, initiate peace, or take responsibility.
3. Let your obedience clear the path for someone else — your step may give courage to those who are watching silently.

Leadership isn't about titles or applause; it's obedience that goes first, integrity that carries weight, and faithfulness that clears the path for others.

Day 30 - Obedience That Changes Direction

Obedience that changes direction means recognising when God redirects your path. It is the humility to adjust rather than push ahead just because you began. Changing direction is not quitting — it is recalibrating.

"Quitting runs from difficulty; redirection responds to guidance."

Sometimes, the signal is a closed door. It can also be repeated resistance, loss of peace, or new clarity from prayer and wise advice. The real question is not, "Did this plan once make sense?" but "Is it still aligned now?"

Many stick to a bad path because of pride, reputation, or fear of looking inconsistent. But obedience values alignment over appearance. God is not tied to your past decisions; He works with your present surrender.

Direction matters more than speed; a slow step on the right path beats fast progress on the wrong one. A small shift today can change a long future.

Think of a budget change. You notice one category draining your finances, so you redirect where your money goes. One small change each month might not seem big, but over time, your finances shift dramatically.

In the same way, obedience often means recalculating before the cost grows too heavy — better to pivot early than to pay later.

Jonah was a prophet — someone familiar with hearing God's voice. But one assignment stretched him beyond comfort. God asked him to go to Nineveh, a violent city, and call its people to change.

"The word of the Lord came to Jonah… 'Go to the great city of Nineveh and preach against it.'" — Jonah 1:1–2

Jonah didn't like the assignment. Instead of going toward it, he went the opposite way and boarded a ship to Tarshish. A storm interrupted the journey, and the ship could not proceed. Jonah was thrown overboard and swallowed by a great fish.

The disruption wasn't random — it was redirection.

Inside the fish, Jonah prayed and realigned his heart. When he was released, the instruction was the same, but Jonah was different. This time, he went to Nineveh.

The result was bigger than Jonah imagined. The people listened, changed, and the city was spared. One changed direction reshaped an entire city.

Jonah's story shows that God's direction can be delayed, but it is not replaced. Realignment still leads to meaningful impact.

Changing direction with God is not failure; it is wisdom. I've had to change direction several times in my life, even when I was already deeply invested. It was humbling to admit I heard God more clearly later than earlier, but that redirection saved me from building a future on the wrong foundation.

Imagine someone who starts a business with great enthusiasm. They invest time, money, and energy. At first, it looks promising, but over time, they sense God nudging them elsewhere — perhaps toward teaching, ministry, or another kind of service.

The temptation is to keep pushing forward because of the investment already made:

- "I've already spent so much money, time, and energy."
- "People will think I failed."
- "I don't want to look inconsistent."

But ignoring the nudge risks pouring years into something misaligned. By contrast, humbling yourself, admitting the shift, and redirecting may open a path of greater peace, fruitfulness, and impact.

That pivot is not failure — it's wisdom. It's like Jonah finally turning toward Nineveh. Redirection didn't erase his calling; it realigned him with it.

Signs You May Need Redirection:

- ***Loss of peace*** - what once felt clear now feels unsettled. Inner restlessness may signal misalignment.
- ***Closed doors*** - opportunities that seemed open suddenly shut. Practical barriers can be God's way of guiding you elsewhere.
- **Repeated resistance** - despite effort, progress stalls. Constant obstacles may indicate you're pushing against God's timing or direction.
- **Fruitlessness despite effort** - you pour in energy but see little lasting impact, suggesting God may want to plant you elsewhere.
- **New clarity through prayer** - fresh conviction or insight emerges, showing a shift in God's leading.
- **Wise counsel confirms change** - trusted mentors or advisors affirm the redirection you've begun to sense.
- **New opportunities align better** - a new path opens that resonates more with your gifts, values, or God's call.

Here are a few ways to work on obedience when direction changes:

- ***Choose Alignment Over Appearance:*** Value God's guidance more than reputation. Redirect when He speaks, even if it looks inconsistent to others.
- ***Respond to Closed Doors with Humility:*** Treat resistance, loss of peace, or shut opportunities as possible signals of redirection. Ask God if the pause is protection.

- ***Practice Recalibration Over Pride:*** Adjust your path instead of pushing forward just because you started. Remember: redirection is wisdom, not failure.
- ***Anchor in Jonah's Example:*** Recall how his detour led to disruption, but his surrender brought impact. Let his story remind you that God's call remains even after delay.
- ***Release "I've Already Invested Too Much" Thinking:*** Refuse to cling to misaligned paths out of fear of wasted effort. Trust that pivoting early redeems time and energy.
- ***Celebrate Small Pivots as Big Futures:*** Reflect at the end of the day on one adjustment you made. Thank God for caring more about your direction than your speed.

The Cost:
1. Letting go of pride about past choices.
2. Admitting a path may be wrong.
3. Releasing "I've already invested too much" thinking.

The Value:
1. A future shaped by alignment, not momentum.
2. Time is redeemed instead of wasted.
3. Impact that comes from accuracy

Reflection:
1. Where might God be prompting a course correction?
2. Are you holding a path just because you started it?
3. What feels harder — changing direction or staying misaligned?

Today's Step:

1. Ask yourself honestly: "Is there any area where I need to change direction?"
2. If something comes to mind, write one small adjustment you can make this week.
3. Act on it. Don't wait for perfect clarity. Even small pivots can rewrite big futures tomorrow.

God cares more about your direction than your speed.

Day 31 - Obedience That Multiplies Beyond You

God often works in multiplication, not addition. His way of expanding impact is different from how we measure it. We often think in terms of numbers, size, or visible strength. But God thinks in terms of surrender. What looks small in your hands can become significant in His.

When you release what you have instead of dismissing it as "not enough," you make room for God to expand its reach. A seed looks insignificant until it is planted. A word of encouragement may feel ordinary until it lands in the heart of someone desperate for hope. A prayer whispered in faith may seem small until it becomes the turning point in someone's life.

Your role is participation. God's role is expansion. You are not asked to manufacture multiplication — only to offer what you have.

We wait until we have "more" before we give or act — more time, more money, more confidence, more certainty. But multiplication begins not with surplus but with surrender. God does not ask for what you do not have; He asks for what you are willing to release.

Imagine a teacher who stays after class to help a struggling student, even when they feel tired and unsure if it will make a difference. A friend who listens when they have no perfect advice. Or a person who shares encouragement while they themselves are still healing.

These moments remind us that obedience is not about scale but about surrender.

They may feel that they are giving little or nothing, yet that small act can shift someone's direction, restore hope, or answer a prayer they never knew about.

A small act surrendered travels further than a large act controlled. What you hold tightly remains limited. What you place in God's hands becomes limitless.

This pattern is seen clearly when Jesus fed five thousand people. He had been teaching near the Sea of Galilee, speaking about the Kingdom of God and healing the sick. Crowds followed because they had seen His works and wanted to hear Him.

By evening, around five thousand men had gathered, not including women and children. The actual crowd was much larger, perhaps ten to fifteen thousand people in total. They were in a remote place, far from resources. People were tired, hungry, and restless.

The disciples, overwhelmed by the scale of need, suggested sending everyone away to find food for themselves. Jesus responded with a challenge: ***"You give them something to eat."***

The disciples quickly calculated the cost and realised it would take more than half a year's wages to feed such a crowd. In other words: impossible. Their eyes were fixed on scarcity, not possibility.

Then Andrew noticed a boy with a small meal — five barley loaves and two fish. Barley bread was the food of the poor, ordinary and unimpressive. It was a simple packed lunch, not a feast. Andrew voiced the obvious:

"Here is a boy with five small barley loaves and two small fish, but how far will they go among so many?" — John 6:9

The boy was unnamed. We know nothing about his background, his family, or his motives. But one detail stands out: he allowed what he had to be placed in Jesus' hands.

That act of surrender became the turning point. The miracle did not begin with abundance; it began with availability.

"Jesus then took the loaves, gave thanks, and distributed to those who were seated as much as they wanted." — John 6:11

The food multiplied as it was shared. Everyone ate as much as they wanted. This was not rationing — it was fullness. No one left hungry, and no one was limited to "just enough." The miracle was abundance, not scarcity.

After everyone had eaten, twelve baskets of leftovers were gathered by the disciples. The detail is striking: not only was the crowd fed, but there was overflow. What began as a boy's small lunch ended as a feast with more remaining than what was first offered. God's multiplication always exceeds human calculation.

The boy did not feed the crowd. He did not plan the miracle or manage the distribution. He simply offered what he had. The multiplication was never his job — it was God's. His obedience was participation, not production.

The boy's act reminds us that obedience is not measured by size but by surrender. What seems ordinary in your grasp becomes extraordinary when placed in God's hands.

Here are a few ways to work on obedience that multiply beyond you:

- ***Offer What You Have:*** Give your time, words, skills, or resources, even if they feel small. Multiplication begins with surrender, not surplus.
- ***Release the Outcome:*** Place your offering in God's hands without tracking or controlling results. Trust His expansion beyond your reach.
- ***Choose Surrender Over Scarcity:*** Refuse to label your gift as "not enough." Remember: a seed looks insignificant until it is planted.
- ***Anchor in the Boy's Example:*** Recall the five loaves and two fish. His small act of surrender became a feast for thousands. Let his obedience inspire yours.

- ***Practice Participation, Not Production:*** Recognise that multiplication is God's role, not yours. Your responsibility is to release; His is to expand.
- ***Celebrate Overflow Beyond You:*** Reflect at the end of the day on one small act you offered. Thank God for the unseen ripple it may create in lives you may never meet.

The Cost:

1. Letting go of the fear of "not having enough.
2. Releasing control over results.
3. Giving even when it feels minimal.

The Value:

1. Impact that exceeds your capacity.
2. Participation in something larger than you.
3. Trust that grows through action.

Reflection:

1. What do you label as "too small" to offer?
2. Where are you waiting to feel sufficient before starting?
3. What might change if you offered what you already have?

Today's Step:

1. Give one small gift today — your time, attention, skill, or encouragement.
2. Release it freely without tracking or controlling the result.

3. Trust God's multiplication, knowing even small offerings can become large outcomes in His hands.

Release your responsibility and trust God's ability.

Day 32 - Obedience When Odds Are Unequal

Obedience in tough times means following God's guidance even when the odds look stacked against you.

It is choosing to move forward when logic says stop, when resources look too few, and when support feels absent. Feeling underqualified, under-resourced, unsupported, or uncertain is not failure — it is often the very environment where God's strength is revealed.

Most people wait until the odds look favourable before they act. They want majority approval, a visible advantage, or a guarantee of success. But obedience does not wait for numbers to line up. It acts on God's instruction first and lets outcomes follow. It shifts the question from "Do I have enough?" to "Did God direct this?"

This kind of obedience does not ignore reality — it simply refuses to make reality the final authority. It acknowledges the facts but trusts God's word above them. It is trust over gains, alignment over chances, and faithfulness over comfort.

Unequal odds are not a barrier — they are a stage. They set the scene for God's power to be displayed, where human strength cannot take the credit. When the odds are against you, obedience becomes the lever that moves what you cannot move alone.

Picture standing at the edge of a challenge that feels far too big. The numbers don't add up. The resources don't match the need. The support seems too thin. Everything in human calculation says, "This won't work." Yet obedience is stepping forward anyway — not because the odds are favourable, but because God has spoken.

Unequal odds magnify the contrast between human limitation and divine strength. They strip away the illusion that success depends on you alone. They create space for God's intervention to be unmistakable. Every step of obedience becomes a declaration: "I trust God more than I trust the math."

Obedience is doing what God asks, even when the math says it shouldn't work. It is stepping forward when the path looks impossible, believing God's direction carries more weight than human calculation. It is choosing His word even when logic, probability, and circumstance argue against it.

This obedience is not reckless — it is rooted in trust. It does not deny reality, but it refuses to let reality be the final authority. It acknowledges the facts yet places faith in the One who stands above them.

And here's the paradox: the smaller the odds, the greater the stage. The weaker the setup, the clearer the miracle. The more unequal the situation, the more undeniable God's power becomes.

Scripture gives a vivid picture of this principle in Gideon's story. Israel was oppressed by the Midianites, whose armies swarmed the land like locusts. They destroyed crops, stole resources, and forced God's people into hiding.

When God called Gideon, he did not see himself as strong. He described himself as the least in his family, from the weakest clan. Yet God gave him an assignment: confront Midian.

Gideon gathered 32,000 men — already small compared to an enemy described as countless. But God said the army was too large.

"The Lord said to Gideon, 'You have too many men. I cannot deliver Midian into their hands, or Israel would boast against me, saying, 'My own strength has saved me.'" — Judges 7:2

Step by step, God reduced the army until only 300 men remained. Human logic saw disaster. God saw the perfect setup.

Instead of swords and shields, Gideon's men carried trumpets, jars, and torches. At God's signal, they surrounded the camp, broke the jars, raised the torches, and sounded the trumpets. Confusion spread. The enemy fled and turned on one another. The victory came without a conventional battle. It came through obedience to instruction.

When God reduces what you rely on, He reveals what you should rely on. What feels like loss is often preparation. What looks like weakness is often positioning. Unequal odds are not a mistake — they are the very conditions where His strength shines brightest.

Gideon's victory was not about numbers, weapons, or human strategy. It was about obedience. Thirty-two thousand soldiers looked small against Midian's countless army, yet God cut them down to three hundred. Human logic saw disaster. God saw the perfect setup. The outcome proved that His direction carries more weight than human calculation.

The jars, torches, and trumpets were not weapons of war; they were symbols of trust. When Gideon's men obeyed the signal, confusion spread through the enemy camp. What should have been a defeat became a victory. What looked like weakness became strength. What seemed impossible became undeniable.

Here are a few ways to work on obedience when odds are unequal:

- ***Choose Instruction Over Logic:*** Act on God's word even when the math says it won't work. Let His direction out-weigh human calculation.
- ***Move Forward Without Majority Approval:*** Refuse to wait for numbers, support, or a visible advantage. Step in faith even when you feel outnumbered.

- ***Practice Trust Over Comfort:*** Acknowledge reality but refuse to let it be the final authority. Place confidence in God's strength above circumstance.
- ***Anchor in Gideon's Example:*** Remember how God reduced his army to 300 men so victory could reveal divine power. Let weakness become the stage for His strength.
- ***Release Dependence on Resources:*** Stop waiting for "enough" before obeying. Offer what you have, trusting God to multiply effectiveness.
- ***Celebrate Courage in Unequal Odds:*** Reflect at the end of the day on one step you took despite resistance. Thank God for proving His strength where yours was limited.

The Cost:

1. Moving forward without a visible advantage.
2. Letting go of majority approval.
3. Trusting instruction over logic.

The Value:

1. Confidence rooted in God, not numbers.
2. Courage that is formed through dependence on God.
3. Victories that point beyond yourself.

Reflection:

1. Where do you feel outnumbered or under-resourced?
2. Are you waiting for better odds before moving?
3. What if the smaller setup is intentional?

Today's Step:

1. Write down one area where the odds feel against you.
2. Identify one step God is asking you to take.
3. Act on it within 24 hours.

If God directed it, the odds don't get a say.

PART VI — BEYOND THE JOURNEY

Day 33 — Obedience as a Lifelong Posture

This is Day 33 — the close of a journey, but the beginning of a lifestyle. You have not simply completed a devotional; you have transformed.

These past 32 days were not just about practice; they were about recalibration. Every reflection, every act of surrender, every step of obedience has been shaping something deeper than habit — it has been forming identity.

Obedience is no longer a practice; it is your posture. Your "Yes" is now settled.

You have been training your heart to respond to God's voice. At first, obedience may have felt like an effort — a conscious decision you had to wrestle with. But now, it has become a rhythm. What began as discipline has become direction. What felt like repetition has become reflex.

Obedience as a lifelong posture means it is not just a momentary choice. It shapes how you stand, think, choose, and respond. It is not an event but a stance. Not a season but a way of living. It means your heart stays positioned toward God, ready to move when He speaks.

You are no longer asking, "Should I obey?"

You are asking, "Where is God leading me?"

This is the shift: alignment with God has moved from decision to default, from effort to identity.

Like a compass, these 32 days have recalibrated your inner needle. Once, emotions, fears, and impulses pulled you in many directions. You may have felt scattered, uncertain, or reactive. But now, your needle rests steady on True North.

The power of a compass is not in controlling the terrain; deserts, mountains, storms, or valleys will still come. Its power lies in keeping direction clear regardless of conditions. In the same way, obedience does not remove challenges, but it ensures you remain aligned. You don't have to obsess over every step; you simply need to check alignment. When the needle points to God, you can walk forward with confidence.

Direction becomes more trustworthy than emotion. Alignment becomes more reliable than circumstance.

Consider a professional athlete after an intensive training camp. They don't finish and return to old habits. The discipline they practised has become an identity. They don't train hard to become athletes; they train hard because they are athletes.

In the same way, obedience stops being a task and becomes identity. You don't obey to prove something; you obey because this is who you are.

Training produces strength, but identity produces consistency. Athletes don't question whether they will train tomorrow — it is simply part of who they are.

Likewise, obedience is no longer a question of "Should I?" but a settled posture of "Yes, Lord."

In the Garden of Gethsemane, Jesus faced the greatest pressure any human could bear. The weight before Him was immense: betrayal, suffering, the cross, and the burden of humanity's sin. His body longed for escape, His soul was overwhelmed with sorrow, and His mind knew the cost. Yet in that moment of agony, His lifelong posture was revealed. He prayed:

"Father, if you are willing, take this cup from me; yet not my will, but Yours be done." — Luke 22:42

This was not a last-minute decision. It was the fruit of a life already aligned. His heart was trained towards the Father in every moment, leading up to this one.

Therefore, when the pressure reached its peak, His response was not hesitation but surrender: *"Not my will, but Yours be done."* Jesus did not just change His circumstances — He changed history. His surrender broke the power of sin and death. It opened the way for redemption. The alignment of One Life released grace for millions.

Gethsemane shows us that we are not tested in comfort but in crisis. It is not proven by ease but by surrender under the weight. Jesus' "Yes" was not situational; it was settled.

Here are a few ways to work on obedience as a lifelong posture:

- ***Choose Alignment as Identity:*** Stop treating obedience as practice. Let it become your default stance, shaping how you think, choose, and respond.
- ***Live With a Settled "Yes":*** Move from asking "Should I obey?" to "Where is God leading me?" Let surrender be reflex, not hesitation.
- ***Practice Compass-Checking Over Emotion-Flow:*** Like a compass pointing to True North, keep your heart aligned with God regardless of terrain, storms, or valleys.
- ***Anchor in Jesus' Example at Gethsemane:*** Remember His prayer: "Not my will, but Yours be done." Let Jesus' lifelong posture of surrender inspire you every day.
- ***Release Independence for Trust:*** Stop clinging to the illusion of self-direction. Allow God's will to guide outcomes beyond your control.
- ***Celebrate Obedience as Identity:*** Reflect at the end of the day on how obedience has shifted from effort to rhythm. Affirm aloud: "My Yes is settled."

The Cost:

1. Releasing the illusion of total independence.
2. Surrendering the right to self-direct every outcome.
3. Choosing God's will over personal preference.

The Value:

1. Stability in decision-making.
2. Authority that flows from alignment.
3. Peace that comes from clarity of direction

Reflection:

1. How has your understanding of obedience changed since Day 1?
2. Where have you seen alignment bring peace, clarity, or a breakthrough in these 33 days?
3. What posture do you want to carry forward into the rest of your life?

Today's Step:

1. Review your 33-day journey and identify the day that stretched you most.
2. Within 24 hours, repeat that action — not as practice, but as posture.
3. After completing the action, in a quiet place, affirm aloud: "I am no longer practising obedience; I am living in alignment with God. My Yes is settled."

Stay aligned, and your life will keep moving toward purpose — one surrendered Yes at a time.

Epilogue — Beyond the Journey

Sustaining Alignment and Obedience Beyond

You didn't just finish a book; you completed a recalibration. In the past 33 days, you've let go of forcing outcomes. Instead, you've embraced the clarity of divine alignment. What you've gained is not a one-time insight — it's a frequency you must remain tuned to for the rest of your life.

Sustaining this alignment requires a fundamental shift in how you approach each day. You are no longer someone trying to be obedient; you are someone who is aligned. The biggest risk after a breakthrough is falling back into old habits — striving, comparing, rushing, or doubting. The power is in the staying — alignment is not maintained by momentum alone, but sustained by vigilance.

To remain in the flow of the harvest, you must guard your "Yes" with greater vigilance than you did on Day 1. The power is in the staying. Alignment is a daily choice. It means keeping your rudder aimed at True North, no matter how far you've come.

Anchors for Daily Alignment:

- Begin with surrender: Each morning, whisper a simple prayer, "Lord, my 'Yes' is already Yours."
- Check your compass: Pause during the day to ask, "Am I still pointing to True North?"

- Close with reflection: End each evening by noting one moment where obedience brought peace or clarity.

Guarding Your Yes:

- Protect it from distraction: Don't let busyness or noise drown out God's voice.
- Resist compromise: Obedience is not partial; it is whole.
- Delay nothing: A delayed Yes often becomes disobedience. Respond promptly when God speaks.

Strengthening Identity:

- Visible reminders: Write "My Yes is settled" somewhere you'll see daily — in a journal, on a card, or as a note on your desk.
- Community support: Share your settled Yes with a mentor, friend, or group. Accountability strengthens posture.
- Return to Gethsemane: When pressure rises, recall Jesus' prayer. Let His example remind you that obedience under the weight of any situation is obedience that changes history.

Day 33 was not the end of a journey; it was the beginning of a new lifestyle. Your 'Yes' is settled. Your compass is steady. Your identity is aligned.

From this point forward, obedience is not something you practice; it is the direction you live from. Stay aligned, and your life will keep unfolding into purpose — one surrendered Yes at a time.

Daily vigilance keeps you aligned; ongoing principles keep you growing. Together, they ensure your Yes remains strong.

Next Steps: Ongoing Principles

This journey was your training camp; now the real mission begins. To help your seeds grow and thrive, create a structure that supports your new identity. These three pillars will sustain your posture of alignment:

- ***Journaling: The Evidence of the Harvest***

Never rely on memory alone to track the faithfulness of God. Continue recording your "Alignment Score" and the daily evidence of obedience. Each entry becomes a testimony of trust.

When the next dry season comes, your journal will be what you draw from. It will stand as proof that the system works. Alignment and obedience don't rely on circumstances; they produce fruit over time, even when things seem barren.

- ***Mentoring: The Law of Multiplication***

Chapter 31 revealed that obedience multiplies when it is shared. You now carry a level of clarity that others around you are quietly starving for. You don't need perfection to mentor — only proximity. Being one step ahead is enough.

Find someone who feels stuck — a younger sibling, a coworker, or a friend. Then, show them the map. Teaching alignment doesn't dilute it; it deepens it. Multiplication is the natural rhythm of obedience.

- **Service: The Rhythm of the Flow**

Obedience is a river, not a reservoir. When service stops, stagnation begins. Remain in the yeast posture — serving quietly, where no recognition is offered. This keeps your ego small and your impact expansive.

Consistent service positions you to receive the next instruction. Flow is maintained by movement.

When you serve, you stay in rhythm with God's purposes, and your obedience remains alive, active, and fruitful.

Final Mandate — The Settled Yes

As you close this book, do not see this journey as a challenge you survived. See it as the moment you stopped fighting the wind and learned how to use it for lift. The map is now in your hands — but the Pilot remains at the controls.

You are no longer grounded by the friction of self-effort. You are positioned to soar. Your life is no longer a struggle for speed; it is a masterpiece of alignment.

Go forth and live a life that heaven itself can describe in one word: ***OBEYED.***

Thank You for Reading

If this book encouraged or strengthened your walk with God, consider leaving a short review where you purchased this book.

Your review helps this message reach readers who may need encouragement in their own season.
Thank you for walking this journey with me.

— Prisca Noronha

About the Author

Prisca Noronha is a Christian author dedicated to helping readers discover peace, purpose, and a deeper walk with God. Through her transformative faith reflections, Prisca inspires intentional living and spiritual growth. Her writing empowers readers to embrace biblical integrity, shaping leadership and service in the rhythms of daily life.

Through biblical reflection and practical insight, Prisca writes for individuals navigating life transitions, seasons of waiting, and the desire to live with meaning rather than pressure. Her writing combines spiritual depth with real-world application, encouraging readers to cultivate consistency, resilience, and a deeper walk with God.

Her debut book, *Obeyed: A 33-Day Devotional to Reclaim Peace, Stop Striving, and Walk in Divine Alignment*, leads readers through a structured journey of faith, surrender, and renewal through daily practice.

Beyond devotional writing, Prisca is developing future works centred on alignment in service, leadership and meaningful human connection — extending spiritual principles into professional and everyday life.

Guiding hearts from pressure to peace through daily alignment.

www.ingramcontent.com/pod-product-compliance
Lightning Source LLC
Chambersburg PA
CBHW062107160726
48282CB00026B/701